Cross Examination

A Primer for the Family Lawyer

Stephen Gassman

AMERICAN BAR ASSOCIATION
Section of Family Law

Cover design by Cory Ottenwess/ABA Design

The materials contained herein represent the opinions of the authors and/or the editors, and should not be construed to be the views or opinions of the law firms or companies with whom such persons are in partnership with, associated with, or employed by, nor of the American Bar Association or the Section of Family Law unless adopted pursuant to the bylaws of the Association.

Nothing contained in this book is to be considered as the rendering of legal advice for specific cases, and readers are responsible for obtaining such advice from their own legal counsel. This book is intended for educational and informational purposes only.

Printed in the United States of America.

21 20 19 18 17   5 4 3 2 1

Library of Congress Cataloging-in-Publication Data
Names: Gassman, Stephen, author.
Title: Cross examination / Stephen Gassman.
Description: Chicago : American Bar Association, [2017] | Includes
   bibliographical references and index.
Identifiers: LCCN 2017044844 | ISBN 9781634255653
Subjects: LCSH: Cross-examination—United States
Classification: LCC KF8920 .G37 2017 | DDC 347.73/75—dc23
LC record available at https://lccn.loc.gov/2017044844

Discounts are available for books ordered in bulk. Special consideration is given to state bars, CLE programs, and other bar-related organizations. Inquire at Book Publishing, ABA Publishing, American Bar Association, 321 N. Clark, Chicago, Illinois 60610-4714.

www.shopABA.org

Table of Contents

CHAPTER 3
Additional Commandments
of Cross Examination   15

CHAPTER 21
Cross Examination of Experts   93

About the Editor

STEPHEN GASSMAN is the senior partner in the firm of Gassman Baiamonte Gruner, PC, Garden City, NY, which limits its practice to matrimonial and family law. He is a graduate of the University of North Carolina and New York Law School.

Mr. Gassman is a Fellow of the American Academy of Matrimonial Lawyers; he has served as President of the Bar Association of Nassau County, New York and Chair of the Family Law Section of the New York State Bar Association. He is a member of the statewide Matrimonial Practice and Rules Committee of the Unified Court System of the State of New York. He has also served as Chair of the Matrimonial & Family Law Committee of the Nassau County Bar Association, as President of the Nassau County Bar Association, and as an Adjunct Professor of Law at Touro Law School, teaching Advanced Family Law. Mr. Gassman has also served as a member of the Judicial Hearing Officer Screening Committee for the Second Judicial Department, a member of the Advisory Board of the Safe Center, and a member of the Law Guardian Advisory Committee for the Tenth Judicial District.

Mr. Gassman has co-authored with Timothy M. Tippins Evidence for Matrimonial Lawyers and Matrimonial Valuation. He has also co-authored with Rosalia Baiamonte the *Library of New York Matrimonial Law Forms* published by the New York Law Journal Press.

He has been a lecturer at matrimonial law seminars and symposiums conducted under the aegis of the New York State Bar Association, American Academy of Matrimonial Lawyers, *New York Law Journal*, NYS Bar Association, American Bar Association, Nassau County Bar Association, Suffolk County Bar Association, Kings County Bar Association, Office of Court Administration—Judicial Seminars, Westchester County Bar Association, Appellate Division Second Department, Association of the Bar of the City of New York, New York County Lawyers Association, Matlaw Systems, New York State Trial Lawyers Association, Family Court Law Guardian Seminars—Tenth Judicial District; and numerous other bar groups.

Stephen Gassman has been listed in The Best Lawyers in America for over 30 years, and has been listed in New York Super Lawyers since its inception in 2007. He has been a guest on and moderator for television shows dealing with matrimonial law on *Court TV* and *Lawline*.

Additionally, Mr. Gassman has had bestowed upon him the award of "Distinguished Past President" by the Nassau County Bar Association, and the award "Education Partner" by Nassau Boces.

Mr. Gassman is the founder of the We Care Fund, the charitable arm of the Nassau County Bar Association, and was the first recipient of the award honoring extraordinary service to this charity—the award is known as the Stephen Gassman Award.

Mr. Gassman is married and has three children and four grandchildren.

1

Introduction

It has been said that becoming a "great" cross examiner cannot be taught, just as becoming a "great" singer cannot be taught, since the attainment of greatness requires innate talents that relatively few possess. Perhaps that is so. What is important to the practitioner, however, and particularly those of us without the innate genius, is that we can learn to be competent cross examiners, so that cross examination advances rather than detracts from our case.

Cross examination can make or break your case and thus it presents the most lethal double-edged sword in the trial lawyer's arsenal. It is clearly the most daunting aspect of the trial. What follows in this book is an attempt to provide the practitioner with lessons, tips, and strategies which are the variegated result of lessons learned the hard way (through mistakes), observations from numerous trials, and the study of the art and science of cross examination.

John Wigmore, an early expert in the law of evidence, described cross examination as "the greatest legal engine ever invented for the discovery of the truth."[1] For our purpose, to learn how to cross examine, we will focus on a somewhat less lofty goal, and look at cross examination as a communication and persuasion contest involving the lawyer, the witness, and the trier of fact. In short, we'll look at how you can use cross examination to convince the trier of fact of the rightfulness of your cause and simultaneously weaken the position taken by the opposing side.

No pride of originality is offered as the substance of this book. It is an amalgam of advice from leading trial lawyers, published works, and

---

1. J. WIGMORE, EVIDENCE §1367 (J. Chadbourn, rev. 1974).

personal experience. As someone once quipped, "plagiarism among lawyers is called research."

Jury versus Bench Trials

The preponderance of the material contained herein applies equally to jury trials as well as bench trials, although at times, suggestions which are posited for dramatic effect need to be tempered somewhat during a bench trial. Nevertheless, the practitioner should be cognizant that in judging the facts of a case, and assessing credibility, judges—like lay jurors—are human and react to the same stimuli and perceptions common to the human experience. They observe the intonations, the body language, and the demeanor of the witnesses and assess reliability and credibility, just like the rest of us.

An advantage that family law practitioners have in generally conducting bench trials, as opposed to jury trials, is the opportunity to know and learn in advance the characteristics of the particular judge—his or her disposition, patience (or lack thereof), the "house rules," and other proclivities. We can and should adjust our strategies accordingly. Contrast this to jury trials where the jurors are virtual strangers to the attorneys, save a brief voir dire prior to their selection as jurors.

A caveat: the "rules" and the "do's" and "dont's" contained herein are, of course, like any rules, subject to exceptions, some of which will be discussed. Seasoned veterans of many trials have learned how and when to veer from the established rules and employ the exceptions—particularly the ubiquitous use of leading questions and the total avoidance of any open-ended questions. The neophyte, however, has to walk before she runs and veering from the rules can be a perilous trek. Until you have obtained the requisite judgment and experience through a multitude of trial battles, a more prudent course of action is to adhere to the rules and change course only when totally necessary. Francis Wellman stated it aptly: "The truly great trial lawyer is he who, while knowing perfectly well the established rules of his art, appreciates when they should be broken."[2]

The "Study" of Cross Examination

How can one obtain proficiency at this most difficult art known as cross examination, which has a steep learning curve? Learning from the experiences recited by old warhorses of cross examination, reading transcripts of good cross examinations, and studying the art through seminars and published works is extremely helpful. As helpful as they are, they are learning by vicarious

---

2. FRANCIS WELLMAN, THE ART OF CROSS EXAMINATION 40 (1905).

experience. There is, of course, no substitute for the trial and error of actually conducting cross examinations.

While we can study cross examination, and learn from actual trial experience, nothing can take the place of judgment. It is impossible to script what will happen in a trial with precision, regardless of the amount of preparation. The trial lawyer is constantly called upon to make instant judgment calls. Should I go any further with this witness? Am I opening a door that should remain closed? What is the risk-reward ratio of pursuing a particular line of questioning with this particular witness? These are just a few of the formidable questions that must be dealt with instantaneously. What the trial lawyer will invariably learn is that by trial and error, our judgment improves. As the saying goes, "Good judgment comes from experience, and experience comes from bad judgment."

Cross Examination Contrasted with Direct Examination

Direct examination, when properly done, presents the witness as the center of attention, the star of the show. The lawyer is little more than the director. In direct examination, the lawyer asks the witness a question and the witness then relates facts in response to the question, often in narrative form.

In cross examination, it is the lawyer who is the center of attention, the star of the show, as well as the director of the production. The lawyer chooses the topics of cross examination, determines the length of cross examination, and chooses the sequence of cross examination. In cross examination, the lawyer does not really ask questions. Rather, the lawyer relates facts, posed as questions, with the witness offering affirmation of the fact ("yes" answer) or negation of the fact ("no" answer).

In direct examination, you are *directing* the witness, with the witness being permitted to answer in narrative form. In cross examination, you are *leading* the witness, with the goal of the witness giving a monosyllabic answer of "yes" or "no." Stated otherwise, direct examination builds, while cross examination leads. If performed correctly, in direct examination, you guide the witness; in cross examination, you control the witness.

2

The Commandments of Cross Examination

No treatise, no class, no seminar on cross examination fails to allude to the late Professor Irving Younger whose lectures on trial practice were legendary. Younger promulgated the "Ten Commandments of Cross Examination." These rules are undoubtedly valid today but should be put in perspective. They are guidelines, not immutable edicts carved in stone. A discussion of these Ten Commandments provides, however, a good launch pad for learning the basic tenets of cross examination.

Bear in mind that a number of commentators and experts on cross examination have been critical of the so-called commandments and have suggested that trial lawyers veer from any strict adherence. While clearly the more seasoned trial lawyer will know when to follow or not follow the commandments, the novice would be well served to adhere to these principles unless and until a requisite degree of skill and confidence has been attained.

Be Brief

"Never cross examine any more than is absolutely necessary. If you don't break your witness, he breaks you." – Rufus Choate

"In trial, less may be more, and more may be a bore, or worse." – James McComas, Dynamic Cross Examination 342 (2011)

Ask no unimportant questions on cross examination. Ask only questions that are aimed at the desired result—to advance the theme(s) of your case, or to discredit your opponent's case. Any question that does not advance your case, or impede your opponent's case, is not a "neutral" question. Rather, it hinders your case. The expectation on cross examination is always high. You are going to "destroy" the witness, impeach her credibility, and obliterate the foundations of the adverse party's case. So-called neutral questions are a sign of weakness and of not knowing where you are going.

If you have made the points you have set out to make on cross examination, regardless of the brevity of time, stop and sit down. Filling time with unimportant questions or minutia will dampen the effect of what you have achieved. Moreover, studies have shown that the attention span of the listener is greatest at the beginning and end of cross examination, or, for that matter, any oratorical presentation. A protracted examination, without a purpose, will result in the lessening of attention by the trier of fact. Remember what a preacher once said: "Nobody gets religion after the first 20 minutes."

Some tools to help make a cross examination brief are:

- Eliminate frequently heard prefixes like "Isn't it a fact . . ."
- Eliminate the excessive use of suffixes or taglines such as "Isn't that correct?"
- Use transitions to change topics by simply stating the next topic, e.g., "I want to ask you some questions about your 2014 tax return."

If you use taglines, don't continually and repetitively use the same tagline. Vary the lines—"Correct?" "Isn't that correct?" "True?" "Isn't that true?" "Right?" The staccato questioning of a witness can sometimes make the cross examiner appear cold and overbearing.

Use Short Questions and Plain Words

Cross examination works best when the witness is subjected to a rapid series of short questions. In the discussion of leading questions, we will see that the short questions should first, be leading, and second, should contain no more than one fact per question. The advantage of a short question is that it curtails the opportunity of the witness to volunteer extraneous material, and it helps to adhere to the other commandments of cross examination in that you will be brief, short, speaking in plain language, and not repeating direct examination.

The choice of words used to formulate the question is important. Cross examination is not the venue to show off your extensive vocabulary or elaborate syntax. Complex language and words unfamiliar to the witness lead to confusion, break the rhythm of cross examination, and loosen the reins of control over the witness that are so essential for the lawyer.

If you have caught the witness in a lie, call it a lie or an untruthful statement. Don't call it a prevarication. Asking the witness through a leading question if his statement of fact has no basis is fine. Don't label what the witness said as spurious or specious.

Part of being brief involves establishing reasonable expectations on your cross examination which you have developed through thorough preparation.

If all you believe can be achieved is to neutralize the witness to some extent, do so and sit down. To portray that you are attempting something more devastating, and not reaching your goal, is a failure of cross examination. For example, if you are accusing a witness of lying and do not present a substantial showing that she is lying, you have damaged your case and buttressed the opponent's case. To paraphrase Ralph Waldo Emerson: "If you attack the king, you best kill him."

Ask Only Leading Questions

On cross examination, there are three types of questions the examiner can use:

1. Open-ended questions
2. Leading questions
3. Declarative questions

Open-ended questions are utilized on direct examination when the witness is invited to elaborate and recite a story. On direct examination, the witness is the star and focal point; the lawyer is merely the director who should never be center stage.

On cross examination, the attorney should avoid open-ended questions at all costs, with a few exceptions, which are discussed in the section "Veering from Leading Questions." Open-ended question often contain the words *who, what, how, explain,* or *tell us.* The cross examiner must avoid these words. They allow the witness to narrate, which then results in the examiner losing control over the witness—the cardinal sin in cross examination.

A leading question is a question so worded as to suggest the proper or desired answer or severely limit the universe of possible answers. This is opposed to not only non-leading questions but misleading questions such as the proverbial "Have you stopped beating your spouse?" inquiries. "Did you ever meet Mr. Jones?" is not a leading question and invites the witness to explain or give a narrative answer. "You had a meeting with Mr. Jones, correct?" is a leading question and invites the monosyllabic "yes" or "no" answer.

The use of leading questions is the greatest weapon in the cross examiner's arsenal. Together with a rapid pace to the questions posed on cross examination, it is how the cross examiner gains control over the witness. Control is crucial. You either control the witness or the witness controls you.

The admonition about eschewing questions which are not leading does not mean that the cross examiner never asks non-leading questions. There are times when the witness must give you the answer you want and if she does it in narrative fashion, rather than a monosyllabic response to your leading question, it has greater dramatic effect. For example, suppose you are cross examining a witness about a prior criminal conviction and you are armed with a certified document of the conviction. Ask the witness if she has ever been convicted of a crime; what crime was charged; what crime, if any, she was convicted of after trial or by plea of guilty, etc. If the witness does not set forth the truth, you have the certificate of conviction for impeachment purposes. Similarly, in those situations where you have the witness "on the run" and no possible answer can help the witness, a leading question is not necessary.

Declarative Questions

The declarative question is a type of leading question where the question itself does not merely suggest, but provides the answer. The witness then merely confirms the answer with a monosyllabic response of "yes" or "no." It is the most effective means of conducting a controlled cross examination, as it ties up the witness in a verbal straightjacket.

> *Open-ended question: What was the weather on the night of June 12?*
>
> *Leading question: Was it raining on the night of June 12?*
>
> *Declarative question: It was raining on the night of June 12?*

Although the declarative question appears as a declarative statement, by the sequence and inflection of your voice, the judge, the court reporter, and the witness know it is a question. The advantage of this type of question is that it positions the cross examiner best to tell the story in the manner the cross examiner wants it told.

By asking only leading questions, you are forcing the witness to communicate in a fragmented mode, as opposed to a narrative mode. Studies have shown that witnesses who speak in a narrative mode, which we employ in direct examination, have greater credibility than witnesses who speak in a fragmented mode.

Veering from Leading Questions

As noted, there are times when it is preferable, particularly for dramatic effect, to jettison the leading question mode of examination. Generally, when you are sure of the answer and the effect of the answer will be augmented if the words spew from the mouth of the witness, you can abandon the leading question. In doing so, however, you still frame your question to avoid an answer that gives the witness wide narrative latitude, and the opportunity to expound on a matter of substantial importance. Some examples are discussed next.

Never Ask a Question to Which You Do Not Already Know the Answer

This caveat is so well known it has become almost a cliché. Of course, there are limited exceptions—when the witness on direct has been effective, the cross examination has so far been totally ineffective, and you basically have nothing to lose by taking the dart board approach to cross examination—delving into areas where you are ignorant of the answers with the hope that something will go your way is at times a disheartening but necessary last resort. Throwing caution to the wind, however, can be dangerous. Sometimes it is better to take your punishment, sit down quickly to stop the bleeding, and rely upon developing your direct case to carry the day.

Generally, you are going to ask questions to which you already know the answer, and your cross examination has been structured in a way that the answer almost does not matter. If you expected a "yes" answer to your declarative question, but received a "no" answer, the goal then becomes to disprove the answer or show that the answer is either absurd or implausible.

> *Please tell the court how many times you have testified as an expert witness in a court of law?*
>
> *How much money did you make last year in your role as an expert witness for husbands and wives in matrimonial actions?*
>
> *Doctor, how long has it been since you treated a patient?*
>
> *Doctor, how many times did you unsuccessfully attempt to become board certified in your field?*

Cross examination is not a discovery tool or a place for a fishing expedition. You have long passed that stage of the litigation. As someone once said, "Fishing expeditions in the courtroom rarely land a great catch. You're more likely to experience a 'perfect storm.'"[3]

When you use cross examination as a discovery tool, you are impaired in your ability to ask leading questions as you do not know the answer you seek, and thus you necessarily invite the witness to be a participant in a conversation with you, the antithesis of the role of the witness that we seek—a cameo role in which the witness gives a monosyllabic answer.

---

3. Donn Fullenweider, The Cross Examination of Experts, Chapter 2.

Listen to the Answer

Of all of the "rules," the one that is easiest to master is ironically the one that most neophytes and even some experienced lawyers consistently run afoul. It is essential that the cross examiner listen carefully to the answer to the question asked. Most inexperienced lawyers are either so wedded to a prepared script, or so concerned that they will not know the next question to ask, that they don't listen to the answer to the question they have just posed. Obviously, the answer to your question determines the next question to ask. Additionally, do not assume that the witness will testify exactly as she did during her deposition.

In addition to listening to the contextual answer, the cross examiner must observe the manner of the answer. Carefully watch the witness' demeanor and body language. Was the answer stated with a higher or lower vocal pitch than usual? Did the witness lean back instead of leaning forward, as to make a point? Is the witness breathing more heavily? Is the witness avoiding eye contact with the questioner? Is the witness perspiring? The demeanor and body language can emit signs and signals that clue the cross examiner that a sensitive and possibly fertile area has been reached, requiring further inquiry.

Do Not Quarrel with the Witness

> *"Cross examination is . . . not the art of examining crossly."* – Horace Rumpole (John Mortimer's famed English barrister)

Quarreling with the witness is counterproductive. It is a sign that you have lost or are about to lose control over the witness. If the witness is intractable, employ the techniques described under the section on the intractable witness, without losing your composure. If the witness' answer is patently absurd, implausible, or was such that will not pass any "smell test," that can be a net gain on cross examination, and the absurdity of the answer can be argued in summation or in a post-trial memorandum.

If the question itself is argumentative, you are inviting an equally argumentative answer and you are losing control. For example, questions that are open ended and begin with words such as "Wasn't it unusual for you" or "Would it not have been more prudent of you to" induce argumentative and explanatory answers by the witness—both types of answer are to be avoided on cross examination. Save your arguments for closing; adduce facts from the witness.

An additional danger of quarreling with the witness is the possibility that the witness will then gain the protective cloak of the court, which may interpret the quarreling as an attempt by the lawyer to bully the lay witness.

Avoid overlapping your next question while the witness is still answering the last question you asked. The appearance is that you are trying to cut off the witness and when you do that, the witness is perceived as having greater control over the lawyer than the lawyer has over the witness.

Do Not Permit the Witness to Explain

This caveat is really a corollary to the rule requiring that you ask only leading questions. If you have questioned the witness properly, with only leading questions, you should have foreclosed the opportunity for the witness to give explanations. Your questions should only relate to facts. Never ask for opinions, evaluations, or interpretations.

To avoid giving the witness an opportunity to explain, avoid the use of summary questions such as "so what you are telling the court is . . ." or "in short, you are saying . . ." and so on. Such questions invite the narrative explanatory response that you are attempting to avoid.

A corollary to this rule is that you must not give the witness on cross examination an opportunity to make speeches. You can avoid giving the witness this opportunity if you phrase your questions as suggested herein. If you ask an open-ended question, for example, asking an expert to state the basis of her opinion, you have set the stage for a lengthy speech by the expert who will expound upon whatever she wants to say, and you will be a prisoner to your own question.

Do Not Ask the Witness to Repeat Testimony Given on Direct Examination

A serious mistake that you can make during cross examination is that you not only fail to impeach the witness, advance your theory of the case, or weaken or destroy your adversary's theory of the case; rather, by going through the witness' direct examination without any meaningful impeachment, you reinforce direct examination and give the witness a second bite of the apple to fill in any information the witness forgot to proffer on direct examination. It is obviously better to waive cross examination than to have cross examination serve as a means to buttress the witness' direct examination. Be selective in the topics of direct examination that you wish to probe upon cross examination. If your cross examination is not planned with set goals laid out, often the result is a reinforcement of direct examination—a cardinal sin in cross examination.

A cross examiner can unwittingly cause the repetition of direct examination when transitioning from one question to another. For example, avoid saying to the witness, "You told us on direct examination that on June 12 [such and such occurred]." Rather, say "Concerning your testimony about the events of June 12 . . ." and then ask the question without repeating the substance of the direct examination.

Avoid One Question Too Many

"Once you have hit pay dirt, quit drilling." – Anonymous

The trial lawyer on cross examination walks a tightrope between firmly implanting in the mind of the trier of fact the favorable answer received on cross examination (admission, concession, prior inconsistent statement, answers that are implausible or patently incredible) and not allowing the witness to explain her way out of the damaging statement.

The rule is simple. Make your point, stop, and go on to your next point. Do not gild the lily. One of the most difficult tasks on cross examination, particularly for the neophyte, is setting limits—knowing when to stop probing, employing judgment to know when you have elicited enough favorable testimony and going any further is fraught with peril. There is no need for overkill, particularly in a civil case where the burden of proof is the mere preponderance of the evidence. To attempt to lock down the witness on a point already won is to give the witness an opportunity to improve upon her answer. Chances for comebacks should not exist in cross examination.

The trial lawyer has to assume that the trier of fact, particularly in a bench trial, employing common sense and intelligence, will draw the obvious conclusion from the factual testimony adduced. Attempting to drill home the damaging testimony more than is necessary opens avenues of escape for the witness.

EXAMPLE:

The cross examiner has skillfully brought out the witness' inconsistent statements in her deposition transcript and in her direct examination. Not content with what has been achieved, the examiner then asks as follows, with the resulting answer snatching defeat from the jaws of victory.

Q: Now, Ms. Jones, please tell the court when were you lying under oath: when you testified under oath at the deposition, or when you testified under oath on direct examination?

A: Actually, neither. What I failed to do was catch the mistake in the 300 plus pages of the deposition transcript. I failed to review it carefully enough and I apologize for that. Now I see my error.

-OR-

A: Actually, neither. I specifically told my prior lawyer about that mistake in the deposition transcript but he apparently neglected to make the change that I requested.

A corollary to the "one question too many" caveat, that has sometimes been referred to as the Single Death Rule, is that if you have accomplished a fatal blow, a real coup, be content and sit down. Don't try to kill the witness twice.

There is a famous story about Abe Lincoln who, when a practicing lawyer, was defending a criminal case and when cross examining the prosecution's lone witness, Lincoln established that the witness could not actually have seen the defendant bite off the victim's nose in a brawl. Instead of stopping, however, Lincoln asked the one question too many: "If you did not see him bite off the nose, how do you know he bit it off?" Answer: "I saw him spit it out." Irving Younger advised that the cross examiner should make three points and sit down. While it is hard to place a strict number of points to make, the lesson is clear. No overkill; no gilding the lily.

One error that frequently occurs in cross examination is that that examiner tries to cover too much and doesn't know when to stop. Stated more aptly, the examiner does not have the discipline and judgment that Edward Bennett Williams was noting when he commented that "a measure of a great trial lawyer is what the lawyer leaves in the briefcase."[4]

Save the Explanation for Summation

As already mentioned, elicit facts from your cross examination, and let the arguments await summation, whether in a bench trial done orally or by written memoranda. In fact, all of the testimony you adduce during cross examination should support your themes of the case, and the themes of your case are then accentuated in summation.

---

4. Quoted in Evan Thomas, The Man to See (1991).

3

Additional Commandments of Cross Examination

Preparation, Preparation, Preparation

"Preparation turns nervousness into confidence." – Anonymous

"It's not the will to win, but the will to prepare to win that makes the difference." – Paul "Bear" Bryant

"Failing to prepare is preparing to fail." – John Wooden

This is a commandment that stands by itself. Unless you have thoroughly and painstakingly prepared the case, and are familiar with the entire case, cross examination can easily become a futile fishing expedition. When you have done your homework, you will be able to plan your cross examination in large part even before the witness testifies. The more thorough the preparation, the more you can anticipate in advance what the opposing side will do and argue, and your ability to counter their points successfully rises exponentially.

Unlike direct examination, when you have the advantage of being able to rehearse a witness in advance, such an opportunity is absent in a cross examination, which only underscores the need for meticulous preparation.

Some useful commandments and tips on preparing for and conducting cross examination are examined in this chapter.

Organize

Organize the documents and exhibits you will use on cross examination so that you have immediate access to them. Fumbling through papers during cross examination alters the pace and hinders the effectiveness of the examination. You must have the impeachment material ready in an instant so that the flow is not interrupted. When a lawyer searches for papers in the middle of an examination, even if the search is relatively brief, it seems like an eternity to others in the courtroom. Organization has been called the most neglected form of advocacy. Many trials involve voluminous documents that can be used on cross examination and numerous deposition transcripts and affidavits filed by the parties. Unless you have spent the requisite time and effort to properly organize this mountain of paper, cross examination will not flow rapidly and gracefully, and will be less effective.

If you have adequately prepared, you can generally anticipate the bulk of the direct examination of the opposing witness, and certainly of the opposing party. By being able to anticipate the direct examination in advance, you can plan almost your entire list of points to be covered in cross examination before the direct examination commences. If you are not able to do this, your preparation of the case has a shortcoming.

One strategy many attorneys find helpful is to have ready access to the sheet of documents and exhibits that have been marked for identification and/or received in evidence. The Exhibit Sheet should be on colored paper so you can easily find it from the counsel table. Google and Facebook (because of their ubiquity, they are now used as verbs) every witness. You never know what you can find.[5]

Use Websites

Check the website of individuals and business entities that are involved in the case. The leads that can be derived from these websites are numerous.

---

5. "A plaintiff must give the defendant access to her private postings from two social network sites, Facebook and MySpace, that could contradict claims she has made in a personal injury action. As the public portions of plaintiff's social networking sites contained material contrary to her claims in deposition testimony, there is a reasonable likelihood that the private portions of sites may contain further such as information with regard to her activities and joined in of life, all of which are material and relevant to the offense this action." Romano v. Steelcase Inc., 30 Misc.3d 426, 907 N.Y.S.2d 650, 655 (Sup. Ct., Suffolk Ct. 2010).

Moreover, they are a fertile area for finding admissions that can be used on cross examination.[6,7]

Consult Written Articles

Most experts have written articles in their field. Read the articles and try to acquire transcripts of the witness' past testimony or past expert reports on topics similar to those at issue in the case. Where, for example, you are cross examining a business appraiser, try to find out the capitalization rate she used when valuing a similar type of business or profession, the method of valuation used and the reasons therefore, the reasonable compensation figure used, and source of data used to find the reasonable compensation figure.

Take Notes Sparingly

Don't be a slave to note taking. Many lawyers attempt to write down the witness' entire direct testimony almost verbatim. By doing so, the lawyer loses the opportunity to observe the demeanor of the witness and the reaction of the trial judge. You could miss key witness body language if you are too dedicated to note taking. Lawyers are not scriveners or court reporters. Write key words and phrases. Trust your memory. Only take notes of the direct testimony that will be subject to cross examination, and then attempt to capture the testimony verbatim. If the case calls for it and time permits, get a copy of the transcript of the direct examination.

Don't Be Over-Scripted

Neophytes may be tempted to write out in advance every question they anticipate will be asked on cross examination. While this may operate as a security blanket, it can also be counterproductive, as the examiner may fail to recognize that he or she should ask the next question based on the previous answer, not from the script. The more seasoned practitioner generally only relies upon an outline or checklist for the purposes of planning a cross examination.

Additionally, you should bear in mind that there are occasions where you will have to not only veer from a particular line of prepared questioning,

---

6. New York has taken judicial notice of facts found on websites, including official government websites (*see, e.g.*, N.Y.C. Medical and Neurodiagnostic, P.C. v. Republic Western Ins. Co., 3 Misc.3d 33, 798 N.Y.S.2d 309 [State Department of Insurance for corporate presence in county]; DeMatteo v. DeMatteo, 194 Misc.2d 640, 749 N.Y.S.2d 671 [Surgeon General's report for dangers of second-hand smoke]; Gallegos v. Elite Model Management Corp., 758 N.Y.S.2d 777 [hospital website for asthmatic conditions and causes]).

7. *See, e.g.*, Romano v. Steelcase, Inc., 30 Misc.3d 426, 907 N.Y.S.2d 650 (2010).

but abandon the line of questioning. For example, if you receive a favorable answer before you have completed the predetermined line of questioning, leave that line of questioning and be satisfied with the favorable response. Conversely, when you are getting unexpected answers to a particular line of questioning that you thought would be fairly safe, it might be best to just abandon that line of questioning or you could cause further harm.

Don't Confine Yourself to Notes

Don't feel that you must confine your cross examination to the notes you took on direct. We will discuss different means of cross examination which do not necessarily conform in sequence or topic to the notes you have taken of the witness' direct testimony in Chapters 7 and 8. Cross examination is more than combating what you hear on direct.

Change the Order of Cross Examination

Do not cross examine the witness in the same sequential order of topics as the witness' testimony on direct examination. Assume that the witness has been prepared for direct and that preparation involved discussing Point 1, then Point 2, then Point 3, and so on. Changing the order and sequence of cross examination makes it more difficult for the witness to perform rote recitation of what he or she has been prepared to state.

Additionally, don't start with the last point that was made by the witness on direct examination. That point is fresh in the mind of the witness. Moreover, if you are not successful in impeaching on that point, you will lose the effect of primacy (see Chapter 5) and the cross examination will appear to be little more than a continuation of direct examination.

As we will see in Chapter 5, dealing with the principles of primacy and recency, it is essential to start and end the cross examination on a strong point of impeachment. Accordingly, the sequence should be as follows: Start with an easy but important point of impeachment, one which is unlikely to provoke an objection; then go from the most effective to least effective or significant points of impeachment; and end on the most destructive impeachment point.

Tell a Story

View cross examination as a story—one about the good themes of your case. Every case should have a theme. The theme may be that the defendant's finances are fraudulent; that the plaintiff can be gainfully employed; that the father/mother is a psychological parent of the children; that the father/mother is guilty of alienating the children; and so on. Whatever the theme might be, plan your cross examination (as well as direct) with a view towards promoting that theme. This is one of the reasons why we suggest that you limit both the use of prefatory language in your questions, such as "Isn't it a fact . . ." and the excessive use of taglines such as "Isn't that correct?" You have never heard a good storyteller or raconteur use such phrases to effectively relate stories and anecdotes.

Don't Sweat the Small Stuff

Don't quibble with the witness on small, irrelevant points. When, for example, you impeach with a prior inconsistent statement, only do so with a matter of substance. If the best you can do is to demonstrate a minor inconsistency on an irrelevant point, you will appear to be grasping at straws and the net effect will be to enhance the standing of the witness rather than debasing the witness.

Cross examine on significant matters only. Otherwise, you trivialize your case. Remember that your goal should be to try a "big picture" case, emphasizing the theme(s) of your case. A handy rule is that when you hear something on direct examination and your reaction is "So what?" don't cross examine on that matter.

Observe the Etiquette of Cross Examination

Don't talk above the witness—it will appear that you are bullying him, or that you don't want the witness to be able to finish his answer for fear that the answer will hurt you. As previously noted, talking above the witness is also demonstrative of your lack of control over the witness. While dramatic effect may require changes in the intonation of your voice, you should never demonstrate loss of temper. Appreciate the difference between being tough and mean, being confident and arrogant, and maintaining control versus being dominant. As Francis Wellman said, "Hold your own temper while you lead the witness to lose his."[8]

Don't Call Certain Witnesses

Do not call a witness on your case when you know your adversary will be compelled to call the witness on his or her case. By adhering to this rule, you afford yourself the opportunity of cross examination, and the use of leading questions (and control of the witness), and simultaneously remove that opportunity from your opponent. If you do this successfully, the impact of turning a witness around on cross examination so that you elicit testimony favorable to your case is much greater than eliciting the same testimony on direct examination.

---

8. Francis Wellman, The Art of Cross Examination (1905).

Minimize Bad Parts of the Case

In planning your cross examination, work diligently on ways to minimize the obviously bad parts of your case. You may advance the theory that although your client has committed a wrong, the effect on the opposing side has been greatly exaggerated and is in reality de minimis—an offshoot of the "no harm, no foul" rule. Whatever the bad part is, it does not go away by ignoring it. Minimize it as best you can.

Avoid Glee

When you have landed a significant punch on cross examination, while you may have engaged in certain proper theatrical presentations to arrive at the *coup de grace*, once the debilitating blow has landed, do not gloat. Show no glee. You are the professional just doing your job. (It's a dirty job, but someone has to do it.) Moreover, you do not have time to savor the blow you have landed. Immediately after you have landed the blow, change to a different topic, thus obviating the possibility of the witness attempting to explain or change her answer. The next topic, however, should be a very significant topic. Remember, the credibility of the witness has just been damaged and the timing is advantageous to question the witness on a significant topic in the case.

Don't Assume Every Witness Is a Liar

Your "attack" on cross examination is often not to show that the witness is an inveterate liar, or a scoundrel who would not recognize the truth if it hit the witness in his or her face. There are witnesses who believe that their testimony is both truthful and accurate. Thus, you might base your attack upon the witness' lack of memory, perception, or another mode of impeachment other than attempting to show that the witness has intentionally lied. You are taking the position that although the witness is honest, she is mistaken, and to show that, you may relax in the strict obedience to all of the commandments of cross examination and let the witness talk. Using a tactic of minimal contradiction—not accusing the witness of lying, but of merely being mistaken in her perception or memory—is an easier path to get concessions from the witness.

Be Sensitive about Sensitive Witnesses

There are certain classes of witnesses—the elderly, children, infirm, and disabled—that must be treated more carefully than the average witness. You should take a softer, more empathetic, and tactful approach with these witnesses. This does not obviate the need to impeach, but you should gear impeachment toward showing that the witness, albeit unintentionally, has erred in his or her recitation of the facts.

Rephrase Confusing Questions

If a question you pose is not phrased properly and the witness is confused, don't argue—arguing will cause you to lose rhythm and control. Take responsibility and say something like "Perhaps I didn't phrase that properly, let me put the question a different way . . ." and keep up the pace.

Offer Courtesy Copies to the Court

When using a deposition transcript, a financial document, spreadsheet, or similar document to aid your cross examination, always offer the court a courtesy copy of the document that has been received in evidence and is being used in the questioning. Complicated testimony, such as financial testimony, is at times hard to follow even with the related document in front of you. Imagine trying to make sense of the testimony without the document. You should also do this when you are developing such testimony on direct examination.

Relish the Silence

If a witness upon cross examination suddenly must take pregnant pauses between your question and her answer, you have probably hit pay dirt. Don't press the witness to answer quickly by stating "Did you understand my question?" or words of similar import. Relish the silence and stare at the witness to increase her anxiety. Every witness who delays in answering or is silent loses credibility. Embrace rather than repulse the silence. This is particularly effective when the witness answered all questions on direct examination without hesitation and with alacrity.

Don't Shoot Every Mosquito

Cross examination, like other aspects of the case, should concentrate on the big picture. Try a "big picture" case. Concentrate on building your themes of the case and destroying the opponent's themes, and focus on the substantive issues. Don't use a cannon to shoot a mosquito. Generally, focus on two or three memorable points of direct examination, not a hodgepodge reaction to every point raised during direct examination. It is a rare instance where you will impeach or destroy every salient point the witness has made on cross examination. Address on cross examination only those points that you can attack, thereby preventing the witness from iterating and bolstering the other points of her direct examination. Moreover, don't assume that what was covered on direct examination is a delimiting roadmap for your cross examination. Often, what is *not* covered on direct examination is the most fertile ground for cross examination.

The only time to consider cross examining on minutiae is when you do so to prove an outright lie. Then you are in a position to argue the maxim "Falsus in uno, falsus in omnibus."

Recognize the Importance of Summation

Remember that every case is a series of building blocks, the goal of which is to build a convincing edifice of facts by the end of the case. You are really trying the case to deliver a powerful and convincing summation—whether orally or through a post-trial memorandum.

You start your case with an opening statement—a preview of what will come. The direct and cross examinations are the building blocks and the summation is when everything coalesces and you establish the theme of the case. Accordingly, realize that not every cross examination—and in fact relatively few—land a total knockout punch. The Perry Mason syndrome is what it always was: fiction. Mason never had to deliver a summation because his cases always ended with his cross examination. We, however, don't have spectators in the courtroom rising and yelling "I did it." Rather, we rely upon jabs and counterpunches to carry the day. The extent to which you have impeached the opposing side is highlighted in your summation. As one sagacious commentator stated, "No jewel shines more brilliantly in summation than the diamond that emerges successfully during cross examination from the black coal of adversarial confrontation."[9]

Develop Your Own Style

We learn from watching and listening to trial lawyers who have mastered their craft, each of whom has his or her own style. We can learn techniques, tactics, and methods, but we must practice in our own skin. If you try to copy someone else's style, it will show. You will be unnatural and uncomfortable. If by nature you are meticulous and detailed, use your own style to your advantage. If you are emotional, display that emotion, within reason.

Know How to Handle the "May I Explain" Witness

Every trial lawyer, regardless of how skillfully she frames the leading questions, experiences a witness who insists upon interjecting a question to the

---

9.   Howard L. Nations, *Cross Examination*, *available at* http://www.howardnations.com/wp-content/uploads/2013/08/Crosexam.pdf.

examiner: "May I explain?" When the witness is unduly repetitive in making this request, an aggressive response might be "Excuse me, sir, but the procedure here is that I ask you the questions." Otherwise, a milder response, and something more than a curt "no" should be along the lines of saying "When I am finished, your lawyer can ask you to explain if she chooses," or "I just want to know (slowly repeat your short simple question)."

Don't Conduct a Deposition as a Cross Examination

Many lawyers disagree on the proper conduct of a deposition. Some lawyers use the deposition as a warm-up cross examination and a preview of the trial. They use impeachment material against the adverse party. In part, the theory is that the opposing side will be intimidated and will be more willing to settle the case.

Our view is that it is a mistake to conduct a cross examination in such a manner. While undoubtedly the client will be pleased with the virtuoso performance, confirming to the client that she retained the "shark" that everyone said you were, the celebration will be short lived. In fact, what has transpired is that the opposing side now has advance knowledge of the evidence you will present at trial. In addition to making changes on the errata sheet to the transcript of the deposition, claiming inadvertent mistakes or more accurate refreshed recollection, the opposing side now has the added advantage of months of time to plan how to combat the ammunition you have divulged.

The traditional view of the function of a deposition is twofold: (1) the deposition should be used to pin down the testimony of the witness; and (2) the deposition should be used as a vital discovery device. Instead of attacking the opposing party at the deposition, let the opposing party be as verbose as she wants. The more the witness talks, the more you have learned about her case and the more material is presented for future use on cross examination. For this reason, you can use "why" questions at a deposition. Also, if you really like the answer you receive from the "why" question, you can repeat it on cross examination.

Where you have received answers at the deposition that you know are not accurate and are untruthful, make sure you pin down the testimony so that the prevarication is set forth in a definitive manner, without equivocation. Effectual cross examination is difficult when you have to use equivocal answers.

The deposition also provides you with the opportunity to get the "feel" of the witness. If the witness is argumentative, obnoxious, and arrogant at the deposition, you may plan to "get under her skin" at the trial. If the witness is sheepish with low self-esteem, she may very well be vulnerable to an aggressive cross examination.

Plan "Win/Win" Questions

In planning your cross examination, while we do not advocate over-scripting, you should prepare as many "win/win" questions as possible. This means that you will score points regardless of whether the witness answers "yes" or "no." For example, you may simply ask a psychologist who made no reference to psychological testing in her report and testimony, "You performed psychological testing on the defendant, true?" If yes, attack that she failed to disclose this fact in her report and testimony. If no, attack the methodology as insufficient. You may ask a forensic accountant if he exercised due diligence and followed the standards promulgated in his profession for the particular appraisal assignment. If the answer is yes, attack what he did and did not do to show that in fact he failed to follow the standards. If he answers no, the attack is obvious.

Use Recesses Strategically

All lawyers ask the court for a recess period from time to time. At times these are occasioned by personal necessity; there are, however, strategic considerations in deciding when to ask for a brief recess and when to politely oppose a recess request by the other side or the court. If you are "on a roll" with a cross examination, and the court asks in substance, "Would this be a convenient time to take a break?," there is nothing wrong with requesting just a few more minutes to complete your line of questioning (even if it will take more than a few minutes). You do not want to interrupt the favorable flow. Conversely, when your witness is being torn apart on cross examination, a request for a short recess, if granted, would be helpful for obvious reasons.

With experts, lawyers often ask for the cross examination to start on the following day, arguing that they should be afforded an uninterrupted cross examination. There is merit to this position. In addition, having the night to do additional preparation for cross examination is invaluable. However, there is one situation that can serve as an exception. Suppose the opposing expert's direct examination ends close to the recess time of the court's day. The court may ask you if you want to defer the commencement of cross examination until the following morning. If you do, it is not uncommon for the direct examiner to immediately ask for a "reopening" of direct examination because he has had overnight to remember that he forgot to ask certain questions. By starting cross examination on the evening before, regardless of how briefly you go, you can generally foreclose such a reopening of direct examination.

Use Repetition

The old adage "Repetition is the mother of all learning" is applicable to the examination of witnesses as well. When you have elicited testimony that is damaging to the witness, an effective technique is to use the substance of the damaging testimony as the beginning of a series of subsequent questions, thereby repeating what was damaging to the witness. Suppose you have elicited testimony that shows that the witness' 2015 tax return was false and misleading in a number of respects. Consider asking the following questions:

> Q: When you signed the false tax return, you knew it was false and misleading?
>
> Q: When you signed the false tax return, you did not inform your accountant of the missing and misleading information?
>
> Q: After you filed the false tax return, you have never amended the return in the two years that have expired since the date of filing?
>
> Q: After you filed the false tax return, you annexed it as an exhibit and submitted it to this court, correct?

4

When Not to Cross Examine

"The phrase, 'No questions, Your Honor' is the hallmark of a seasoned pro. It takes more experience, courage, and self-confidence to use this phrase than to follow the natural impulse to dive in." – F. LEE BAILEY, TO BE A TRIAL LAWYER *(1985)*

"More cross examinations are suicidal than homicidal." – Emory Bruckner

Leon Jaworski, of Watergate fame, once noted that the most difficult thing for a lawyer to say is "No cross, Your Honor." The strategic and tactical decision of whether or not to cross examine a witness is a crucial one. You must evaluate the risk and reward. You should not predicate your evaluation upon your desire to show how smart you are, or to appease your client who expects you to cross examine every witness in a style akin to what she has viewed on television.

The first thing to weigh is the fact that after you cross examine a witness, opposing counsel has a chance to redirect and rehabilitate, if necessary. Always weigh the points to be scored by cross examination against the potential for losing points on redirect. If you have listened to direct carefully and detected a major flaw in terms of omission of certain relevant testimony or incorrect testimony which has the effect of advancing your cause, caution may dictate to leave well enough alone and forbear from cross examining the witness. By waiving cross, you deny your opponent the opportunity to correct errors or omissions.

The cross examiner must also make a judgment call on whether he or she can clearly show at least a motive to fabricate and show a substantive line of testimony where there is at least a likelihood that the witness would fabricate. Above all, if cross examination will not help your case, or hurt your opponent's case, don't cross. There are several general rules about when to not cross examine or to severely limit cross examination.

Don't Cross Examine the Harmless Witness

If the witness has not hurt you on direct examination, then there is no reason to cross examine and give the witness a possible chance to augment or change in any respect the harmless direct. This is particularly true when you know that the witness is cognizant of information harmful to your case but due to the ineptitude of counsel and/or the witness, that harmful testimony has not been elicited. Ask no questions and set the witness out of the courtroom as soon as possible.

An exception might be if you are very confident that your cross examination can turn this witness not only into someone who has not hurt your case, but someone who will effectively enhance your case. In our zeal to impeach a witness, we often lose sight of the fact that this witness has information, not imparted on direct examination, which can be of assistance to the cross examiner's case. In effect, you are using an adverse witness to elicit testimony on cross examination that was not elicited on direct examination and which is favorable to your case—a technique sometimes referred to as hitchhiking.

Of course, you should embark upon such a cross examination only if you are confident you can adduce the favorable testimony from the adverse witness. If not, and the witness provides harmful evidence during cross examination, it is similarly much more lethal that if it was adduced during direct examination. In other words, there are no neutral cross examinations. If you don't score the points you seek, you have lost.

Don't Repeat Direct Examination

When all you are going to accomplish is to repeat and thereby reinforce the direct examination, avoid this unnecessary reiteration, and opt out of cross examination.

Don't Clarify the Confusing

At times, the direct examination of a witness is confusing if not outright incomprehensible. The point made here in several places (e.g., the Chapter 7 section titled "Testimony Is Implausible or Unreasonable") is the importance of the trier of fact understanding your case, be it complex expert testimony about esoteric issues or lay testimony with a sequence of events that is difficult to follow because of the manner of presentation. In this instance, leave "bad enough" alone and deny the witness the opportunity to clarify.

When you have made the decision not to cross examine a witness, and the court indicates it is ready to entertain your cross examination, say more than "No questions, Your Honor." State something like "Thank you, Your Honor, but it is not necessary to cross examine this witness," or "We feel no need to cross examine this witness, Your Honor."

A possible, albeit rare, exception to the rules about when not to cross examine may exist if the direct examination has been so devastating to your case, and you have a dearth of impeachment material. Then you may take a chance to cross examine about numerous topics, both direct and collateral. The theory is that you have nothing further to lose and you just might elicit some ameliorating testimony.

5

The Principles of Primary and Recency

In planning cross examination, the examiner must be cognizant of the basic psychological principles of *primacy* and *recency*, which are universally accepted. Simply stated, they are as follows:

Primacy: What we hear first, we tend to believe.

Recency: What we hear last, we tend to remember.

Primacy may be viewed as an offshoot of the old adage "You only have one chance to make a first impression." To take advantage of the principle of primacy, you must begin cross examination with an important and positive form of impeachment, such as a motive of the witness to fabricate or a major inconsistency in the witness' sworn testimony. Generally, the principle of primacy should relate to adducing testimony that affects the witness' credibility. The importance of primacy is that it tends to color, if not taint, our view of what we subsequently hear and see. In effect, the principle of confirmatory bias—the tendency to search for or interpret information in a way that confirms one's preconceptions—also often comes into play.

Studies have shown that the most vulnerable time for a witness who is subjected to cross examination is the first ten minutes. If the cross examiner makes the witness feel uncomfortable, embarrassed, or overly anxious at the beginning of the cross, the witness never relaxes and becomes easier prey.

The principle of primacy is the reason we discourage the use, too often employed by some attorneys, of the language crutches that precede many questions, such as "Isn't it a fact . . ." or "Isn't it true . . ." People tend to listen most carefully to the beginning and end of a particular question. Why waste the apex of the attention span of the trier of fact with a meaningless and

31

unnecessary phrase? Learn to frame questions without these introductory crutches. They are a waste of time and are unnecessary.

Additionally, the principle of primacy is a reason to forego a saccharine salutary introduction to the witness who is about to be cross examined, which are too often used and which, when used, are often much too long. Even a novice lay witness has watched television and knows you are out to destroy her. These types of introductions smack of insincerity and again consume the period of the trier of fact's heightened attention span. Accordingly, you don't need to recite to the witness at the onset of a cross examination the usual phrases: "I am going to ask you certain questions," "If you do not understand the question, please let me know and I will rephrase the question," "We are only seeking the truth in this trial," etc. Do not waste time with these opening salutations.

The principle of recency—what you hear last you tend to remember— often has a greater impact on a final decision. This mandates that you end the cross examination on a high note. Apply the principle of recency not only to the end of the entire cross examination but to the end of breaks in the cross examination, such as lunch breaks or the close of court on a particular day.

The principle of recency is more difficult for the cross examiner to adhere to and requires greater discipline. If you are scoring points at the beginning of the cross examination (primacy), the natural tendency is to continue to use all the good stuff. After all, you are "on a roll." However, you must employ discipline and save the best for the end. A good practice is to select the high point of your cross examination and place it at the end of your cross examination notes.

Another judgment call involved in the principle of recency is to measure whether you should stop a cross examination even before its planned conclusion. For example, if you reach an apex in the examination—you have seriously impeached the witness—you may decide to stop the examination, ending on a high note and employing the principle of recency, even if your planned cross examination called for a continuation of the examination on several other topics. Unless those other topics are very important, stopping on a high note may be the more prudent and effective course of action.

In choosing what to save for the end of the cross examination, consider something that may need explanation or amplification by the facts to be adduced during the course of the cross examination. Having adduced those facts, you can end the examination with a crescendo effect.

Employing these principles, the order of cross examination should be as follows:

> *First: Very strong point*

> *Second: Balance of points from strongest to weakest*

> *Third: The strongest point saved for last*

6

The Use of Trilogies

In speech, in writing, and on cross examination of a witness, the use of a tripartite structure has proven to be an extremely effective form of communication. Three of something—be it clauses, examples, or parallel sentences—provides an effective rhythm and cadence, as well as a sense of completion. Two of something appears oppositional; four of something is tedious and difficult to remember. Three is generally the correct formula to make a particular point. Examples of the effective use of trilogies abound: blood, sweat, and tears; I came, I saw, I conquered; earth, wind, and fire; Father, Son, Holy Ghost.

In a trial setting, trilogies can be used on direct examination, cross examination, and summation. In the latter, the late Edward Bennett Williams, while defending the late Jimmy Hoffa, was discussing in summation a government witness whose credibility was attacked during trial. Instead of simply relating to the jury that the witness was a liar, Williams employed the tripartite structure as follows:

> *From this man's lips, we learned that he lies;*
>
> *From this man's lips, we learned that he deceives;*
>
> *From this man's lips, we learned that he falsifies.*

Note the additional dramatic effect of the trilogy as opposed to a single, simple declarative sentence.

The use of a tripartite structure can be combined with the principles of looping (see Chapter 10) for even more dramatic effect. Suppose at a hearing for contempt for the father's failure to pay child support, where the father has testified on direct that he loves his children dearly, the examiner poses the following questions on cross examination of the father:

> *For the children you profess to love, you refused to pay for their tutoring?*
>
> *For the children you profess to love, you refused to pay not only for their tutoring but their medical bills? (looping tutoring and medical bills)*
>
> *For the children you profess to love, you refused to pay for their tutoring, their medical bills, and their camp? (looping tutoring, medical bills, and camp)*

Consider if these questions are followed by questions with respect to the father's financial contributions to his paramour during the period he failed to pay child support.

> *For your girlfriend, you paid for a ten-day stay in Aruba?*
>
> *For your girlfriend, you purchased a tennis bracelet for her birthday?*
>
> *For your girlfriend, you paid the rent on her apartment in the sum of $3,500 per month?*

7

Modes of Impeachment

There are a number of different modes of impeachment, some of which apply to all witnesses and some of which are endemic to experts. The cross examiner who has carefully planned decides in advance the modes that would be most effective with a particular witness.

Bias, Interest, Motive, and Prejudice

When you can prove bias, interest, motive to falsify, or prejudice in favor of one party or against the other party, it is best if you bring this out at the beginning of the cross examination. The taint on the witness will endure throughout the examination, and you will be starting on a strong point and thereby employing the principle of primacy.

Explore if the witness is a friend, relative, colleague, coworker, or employee of the adverse party and play the relationship out for the maximum effect. Is the witness here voluntarily? What sacrifice(s) did the witness make to come to court? Are the sacrifices made out of friendship or is she being compensated in some manner? Were there prior discussions with the adverse party and/or attorney? And so on. The following questions deal with an employee of the defendant, now being cross examined:

> You are employed by Mr. Anderson, correct?
>
> You have been employed by him for eight years?
>
> You like your job at the corporation Mr. Anderson owns?

(continued)

You believe you are compensated fairly for your efforts?

You have no desire to lose your job?

You want to retain your job?

You support your family with the salary earned from this employment?

You were asked by Mr. Anderson to come to court today to testify?

You immediately replied in the affirmative?

You were not served with a subpoena to come to court, correct?

You came voluntarily after Mr. Anderson asked you to come?

Prior to coming to court, you met with Mr. Anderson's attorney, Mr. Dewey?

You met Mr. Dewey at his office?

You went to Mr. Dewey's office because Mr. Anderson asked you to do so?

An example of a cross examination of a friend who is testifying for the adverse party is as follows:

You are appearing here today voluntarily?

No subpoena was served upon you to appear in court?

You are here because Mrs. Smith asked you to be here?

She only had to ask you once and you agreed to come to court and testify?

To come to court today, you have missed a day of work?

Are you paid for this missed day of work?

Is the missed day of work chargeable to your vacation time?

Did you pay for child care to come to court today?

Did Mrs. Smith reimburse you for this expense or promise to reimburse you?

> She is a friend and neighbor of yours?
>
> Your children are friends with her children?
>
> They regularly play together?
>
> Did Mrs. Smith drive you to the courthouse today?
>
> Is she going to drive you home after the court session is over?
>
> How long was the drive from your home to the courthouse?
>
> Did you talk about the case during this 40-minute drive?
>
> You have spoken to Mrs. Smith's attorney prior to coming to court today? (develop when, time spent, what was discussed, etc.)
>
> Are you here today to be fair and unbiased?
>
> Are you a partisan for Mrs. Smith?
>
> You and I have spoken before this trial, correct?
>
> I called you, introduced myself as Mr. Smith's attorney, and told you I wanted to ask you some questions?
>
> You refused to speak to me?
>
> You did not refuse to speak to Mrs. Smith's attorney?

In a custody case, a nanny may testify for one party. Explore if any threats have been made to the nanny regarding continued employment, or if the nanny's immigration status is in issue and if anyone threated her because of this issue.

Where a relative testifies for a party, e.g., a mother testifying on behalf of her son, there is no harm in the following set of questions:

> You love your son, correct?
>
> That has always been the case?
>
> You have helped you son whenever you could throughout his childhood and now into adulthood?
>
> You want your son to prevail in this litigation, correct?

From an evidentiary standpoint, the collateral evidence rule, extant in many jurisdictions, which interdicts the use of extrinsic evidence to cross examine a witness on a collateral issue for the purpose of impeachment, does not apply to bias, interest, prejudice, and motive. A witness' bias in favor of the party proponent, his prejudice or hostility against the opposing party, or an interest in the litigation are proper avenues of impeachment. Not only may you cross examine the witness with respect to such matters, but, if the witness denies the bias or hostility, you may prove it by extrinsic evidence, because it is not regarded as collateral. Accordingly, if witness A on cross examination denies that she is biased against your client, you are free to call a witness on your case who will testify that witness A is in fact biased against your client and the reasons therefore.

Prior Inconsistent Statements

"You should never hazard the important question until you have laid the foundation for it in such a way that when confronted with the fact, the witness can neither deny nor explain it." – FRANCIS WELLMAN, THE ART OF CROSS EXAMINATION (1905)

The prior inconsistent statement is considered by some to be the holy grail of cross examination. The statement inconsistent with the witness' direct testimony may be in the form of deposition testimony; a prior affidavit of the witness in this action, in some other action, or for some other purpose; a loan application or other financial statement; or a tax return or other document.

To effectively use a prior inconsistent statement, the inconsistency should be one of substance that will affect the credibility of the witness. Making a big deal of a minor inconsistency slows the pace and gives the impression that you really have little firepower for this witness. Focus on inconsistencies that concern important issues in the case.

The paramount consideration in cross examining with a prior inconsistent statement is to have patience and lay the proper foundation before confronting the witness with the inconsistent statement, so as to deny the witness any wiggle room to explain or mollify the effect of the inconsistency. Absolute control of the witness is the rule of the day when impeaching with a prior inconsistent statement. Disaster occurs when in haste, the attorney fails to set up the prior inconsistent statement properly. The result will then likely be that all you have accomplished is to refresh the witness' hazy recollection, or give the witness the "out" of simply stating "I made a mistake in my prior statement."

Additionally, by going right to the prior inconsistent statement without the proper foundation, i.e., committing the witness to her direct testimony, you have lost the dramatic effect that appends the confrontation of the inconsistent statement. The proper methodology can be broken down into a series of steps.

Step 1

Firmly commit the witness to her direct testimony. Question the witness about the relevant direct examination testimony. Do not ask the witness if she "remembers" giving the prior statement, as she might say no. Tell the witness she gave it. Also, don't show the witness the prior written statement until you have to.

A sample set of questions might be as follows:

> *You took an oath when you took the stand and answered questions on direct examination?*
>
> *An oath to tell the truth?*
>
> *You told the truth, correct? (win, win question)*
>
> *You realize the importance of honoring the oath and telling the truth in this forum?*
>
> *You told us in your direct testimony that in the calendar year 2010, your income was limited to a salary from ABC Corporation?*
>
> *And that you had no other sources of income whatsoever?*
>
> *And you are certain of that?*
>
> *You have no doubt?*
>
> *And you have never stated to anyone, verbally or in writing, to the contrary?*

Step 2

Direct the witness' attention to the place and time of the prior inconsistent statement, without yet divulging the statement, and the importance of the prior inconsistent statement.

> *In May of 2009, you purchased a house that you now own and live in, correct?*
>
> *And to make that purchase you applied for and received a mortgage from Chase Bank?*
>
> *As part of the mortgage application you filled out a financial statement?*

(continued)

> *And you submitted that financial statement to Chase Bank in order to induce them to give you a mortgage?*
>
> *You were aware of the importance of this financial statement, were you not?*
>
> *You checked it for accuracy, correct?*
>
> *It was accurate, true?*
>
> *You would not attest to its accuracy if it wasn't true, correct?*

By way of another example, suppose the inconsistency was contained in the transcript of the witness' deposition testimony. You should ask preliminary questions to show the seriousness of the occasion, and the fact that the witness was not caught off guard and had ample time to consider her testimony. The line of questioning might be:

> *You have given prior sworn testimony in this case, correct?*
>
> *You appeared in my office on June 12 for a deposition?*
>
> *You knew weeks in advance of June 12 that you were going to appear in my office for the deposition?*
>
> *You discussed your deposition testimony with your attorney prior to coming to my office, correct?*
>
> *You arrived at my office with your attorney?*
>
> *Your attorney sat by your side throughout the testimony?*
>
> *You saw a court reporter in the room?*
>
> *The court reporter took down every word that was stated?*
>
> *The court reporter administered an oath to you, true?*
>
> *You raised your right hand and swore to tell the truth?*
>
> *Did you tell the truth? (win, win question)*
>
> *Now, I draw your attention to page 23 of the transcript of your deposition, beginning at line 12, where I asked you the following question and you gave the following answer . . .*

When you impeach with a deposition transcript, first offer the court a courtesy copy of the transcript so the court can follow along effectively. Advise the court and the adversary of the page and line number you are reading from. Read the words "question" and "answer" as they appear in the transcript.

Remember that the use of a prior inconsistent statement depends in large part upon the effectiveness of the deposition of the witness. If the witness' answer at the deposition to a particular question is equivocal, the effectiveness of using it to impeach at trial is reduced or eliminated. Accordingly, the deposition must be precise. The deposition is the forum to pin down the witness' testimony, even when and particularly when you know it is false. The deposition is not the place to show off to your client and confront the witness with her false statement, thereby losing the opportunity to do so at trial. From a client relations viewpoint, the client should understand that you don't "win" the case at the deposition; rather you lay part of the groundwork for the win at the deposition.

Step 3

If the prior inconsistent statement is not from a deposition transcript, but from some other document, have the prior inconsistent statement marked for identification and shown to the witness, and use the actual language of the prior inconsistent statement to impeach and drive the inconsistency home.

For emphasis and dramatic effect, after you have impeached the witness with a prior inconsistent statement on a substantive matter, let the inconsistency sink in. Move slowly back to the lectern, and take your time. You might ask the court, "May I have a moment, Your Honor?" Let the trier of fact have time to absorb the import of the inconsistency. Additionally, the next line of questioning should not be about the topic upon which you have just confronted the witness with a prior inconsistent statement. This is necessary so the witness lacks an opportunity through subsequent questions to rehabilitate herself. The topic you choose to continue the questioning should be one of considerable import to the issues in the case. The goal is to hit the witness while she's down. The witness has just been impeached, she's reached the nadir, her credibility is in the basement. It will now be difficult for the witness to give convincing testimony on a crucial issue.

A pitfall to avoid in impeaching with a prior inconsistent statement is using this method of impeachment when the inconsistency is minor and of little, if any, relevance. Also consider avoiding this method when the inconsistency is forgivable, such as an understandable confusion as to dates. In short, the inconsistency must be material.

The most important part of impeaching with a prior inconsistent statement is to close all the escape hatches available to the witness before the witness is confronted with the prior inconsistent statement. Try to imagine how you would try to escape if you were confronted with the subject prior inconsistent statement. Lock in the witness' testimony on direct, show that the witness was serious and prepared in giving the prior inconsistent statement, and then confront the witness with the prior inconsistent statement.

Even when the witness is a party, and the prior inconsistent statement is received as an admission as opposed to just impeachment of testimony, no foundation is required (see Federal Rules of Evidence Section 613(b), infra). The steps contained herein should be followed to effectively use the prior inconsistent statement. Where the witness impeached with a prior inconsistent statement is not a party, you will generally need a proper foundation in order to use the impeaching material.

Federal Rules of Evidence, section 613, entitled "Witness's Prior Statement," provides as follows:

(a) **Showing or Disclosing the Statement During Examination**. When examining a witness about the witness's prior statement, a party need not show it or disclose its contents to the witness. But the party must, upon request, show it or disclose its contents to an adverse party's attorney.

(b) **Extrinsic Evidence of a Prior Inconsistent Statement**. Extrinsic evidence of a witness's prior inconsistent statement is admissible only if the witness is given an opportunity to explain or deny the statement and an adverse party is given an opportunity to examine the witness about it, or if justice so requires. This subdivision (b) does not apply to an opposing party's statement under Rule 801(d)(2). [admission exception to hearsay rule]

In an actual trial, an expert witness was testifying about the husband's enhanced earning capacity, and the cross examiner was familiar with writings by the witness on the subject. The expert witness' direct testimony was diametrically opposed to what the witness had written in a chapter on the subject of enhanced earning capacity. The cross examination, edited for brevity, went as follows:

Q: Mr. Expert, I want to read a sentence to you. [read sentence without attribution]

Q: Did you hear and understand the statement?

Q: Do you agree with that statement?

Q: Have you always disagreed with the substance of that statement?

Q: Would someone who holds himself or herself out as an expert in this field be regarded by you as knowledgeable in the field, based on the substance of that statement?

Q: [Approach the witness and ask him to read the passage from the book and identify the book and the author, i.e., the witness.]

Walk slowly back to the lectern.

STOP

Testimony Is Implausible or Unreasonable

More often than not, instead of showing an outright lie by the witness, the cross examiner will be able to demonstrate that the witness' testimony is not plausible, it strains credulity, or it just does not pass the "smell test" that most of us employ in gauging credibility. By plausibility, we do not mean empirical truth, but rather where the trier of fact thinks the truth lies, generally based upon common human experience. Accordingly, when the witness gives a "bad answer," one that is contrary to common human experience, points have been scored on cross examination. Don't fight the "bad answer," encourage more of them. Let the witness fall off the cliff.

If a witness is an employee of a party, and you ask "Do you want your employer to lose?," any answer other than "no" would seem implausible. If a witness has a financial interest in the outcome of the case, and you state, "Making money is important to you," any answer other than "yes" would be implausible.

From the trial lawyer's point of view, implausible answers on cross examination are okay. It doesn't matter if the answer was truthful or not; the answer was completely implausible even though possibly truthful. The point can be made by considering some well-publicized examples. When Supreme Court Justice Clarence Thomas was going through the Senate confirmation committee hearings, he was asked about the Supreme Court decision in *Roe v. Wade*. Justice Thomas was a law student when that case was handed down by the Supreme Court. He was asked in the confirmation hearings if he ever discussed that decision with anyone. He answered "no." Whether or not truthful, for someone who was a law student when this momentous decision was made and went on to become a federal judge to deny any discussion about the case is not plausible. Similarly, and on the other side of the political spectrum, President Clinton's admission that he smoked marijuana but did not inhale is equally implausible, regardless of whether truthful or not.

In adducing answers that are implausible, the trial lawyer is employing the rule of probability: the trier of fact will question the testimony because it is more probable than not that the facts or conclusions advocated by the witness were not reasonable, plausible, or truthful. To use a common example, suppose in a support case, the payor spouse claims a sudden sharp diminution of income that conveniently occurs at or about the time of the commencement of a matrimonial action—the so-called instant poverty syndrome. A series of questions along these lines may demonstrate the lack of probability of the payor's position:

> Q: Mr. Smith, you have been in this same business for many years, correct?
>
> Q: In excess of 20 years in fact?

(continued)

> Q: You are aware that your income, per your own tax returns for the 19 years prior to the commencement of this lawsuit, was never less than $300,000 per year?
>
> Q: You are aware that this action was commenced on January 30, 2014?
>
> Q: And that was the first year in over 20 years that the income you claimed you earned was less than $300,000?

Bad Reputation in the Community for Truth and Veracity

You can impeach the credibility of a witness, whether a party or not, in both civil and criminal cases, by showing their reputation for truth and veracity is bad. To do this, you must lay a proper foundation showing that a key opposing witness has a bad reputation in the community for truth and veracity. While often used in criminal cases, this mode of impeachment is too often ignored in civil cases.

Pursuant to this rule, a party has a right to call a witness to testify that an opposing witness, who gave substantive evidence and was not called for purposes of impeachment, has a bad reputation in the community for truth and veracity. Whether the opposing party may, in turn, call witnesses to rebut the testimony of the impeaching witness is generally an issue resting in the discretion of the trial court.[10]

The use of such a witness is not deemed collateral. The cross examiner does not seek to contradict specific answers given by witness, but, rather, seeks to show that the witness has a bad reputation in the community for truth and veracity.

Prior Criminal Convictions

You may cross examine a witness with respect to specific immoral, vicious, or criminal acts which bear upon the witness' credibility. Generally, the nature and scope of such cross examination is discretionary with the trial court. However, the inquiry must have some tendency to show moral turpitude to be relevant to the credibility issue. There are certain generally accepted limitations with respect to this mode of impeachment:

- Cross examination relative to specific misconduct must be based upon reasonable grounds and pursued in good faith.

---

10. *See, e.g.*, People v. Pavao, 59 N.Y.2d 282, 288, 464 N.Y.S2d 458 (1983).

- A witness may not be asked about conduct which was the subject of criminal charges when those charges resulted in an acquittal.
- An adverse party or a hostile witness may not be impeached on direct examination by evidence of his or her criminal conviction.

Federal Rules of Evidence, section 609, provides for use and limitations on past criminal convictions as a basis for cross examination.

Lack of Knowledge

Some witnesses simply lack a bedrock of knowledge about the facts being testified to, or lack knowledge of the subject matter of the lawsuit. Many lawyers are cognizant of the cross examination of Woody Allen when he was engaged in a child custody battle with Mia Farrow. The cross examination consisted of a series of questions about the routine, likes, and general life of his child, about which he was largely unaware. This type of attack has been used in other custody cases where the party seeking custody, possibly for less than valid reasons, is not familiar with many aspects of the child's life. Possible questions include:

> *What is the name of your daughter's teacher?*
>
> *What was the name of your daughter's teacher last year?*
>
> *What is the name of your daughter's best friend?*
>
> *What was the last book your daughter read?*
>
> *What is her favorite color?*
>
> *What does she call the doll she sleeps with?*

Other Modes of Impeachment

Areas open for impeachment include, among others, the following:

- Lack of perception. The witness' inability or lack of opportunity to perceive the event about which the witness has proffered testimony. For example, the witness was intoxicated at the time of perceiving the alleged event, the view of the witness was blocked, etc.
- Memory difficulties. The impeachment could focus on the great length of time between the event in question and the giving of testimony, or impairments peculiar to the witness (advanced age, psychiatric history, disease, etc.). Where a witness has testified with certainty and the circumstances suggest the improbability of such a clear and definitive recollection, test the witness' memory about other details that are related to the event.

- Communication difficulties. Possible distorted testimony owing to the witness' lack of effective communication skills.
- In the case of experts, that the expert is not qualified to proffer testimony on the subject in issue, or the expert's opinion is contrary to recognized authority. (See Chapter 21)
- That the testimony of the witness has been coached and rehearsed. When you sense that this is the case, ask the witness to repeat the story. You will almost always get a verbatim iteration. When you question the story out of sequence, however, asking a question about the middle of the story, and then about the beginning of the story, etc., it is more difficult for the witness to stick to the prepared script.

Riding the Lie

When you have caught the witness in a clear lie, it is not running afoul of the "don't gild the lily" concept if you ask safe questions which emphasize the intent and purpose of the lie. The idea is to take a single lie and make the witness appear to be an inveterate serial liar. The goal is for the court to employ the adage "Falsus in uno, falsus in omnibus"—false in one thing, false in everything. Consider the following questions after the acknowledgment of the falsehood:

> Q: This lie was created by you?
>
> Q: You created this lie because it helped you at the time?
>
> Q: The lie that you created helped you in that it made you more money?
>
> Q: You lied when it worked to your advantage?

8

Types of Cross Examination

There are different strategies to use for different witnesses and also for the various parts of cross examination. Which type of cross examination to employ at a given time is a judgment call you will make after thorough preparation.

Constructive versus Destructive Cross Examination

In destructive cross examination, you seek to destroy the credibility of the witness and limit the effect of the witness' direct testimony. To do so, you use the various modes of impeachment discussed in Chapter 7. As a substitute for or in conjunction with destructive cross examination, you employ constructive cross examination, which is designed to elicit helpful testimony from a seemingly adverse witness. The constructive nature of such a cross examination can take several forms.

First, you may use the adverse witness to corroborate certain points that have been made or will be made by your witnesses. Often, the witness being so cross examined is not cognizant that she is corroborating testimony adduced or to be adduced by the opposing side. Using this type of cross examination may also obviate the necessity for your side to call one or more witnesses.

Second, you can use the adverse witness to concede points that are favorable to your case. Think of ways to use your opponent's witness to advance your theory of the case. Often this entails questioning such a witness about matters that were not reached during direct examination. Again, the witness may be helping your case without realizing she is doing so. By this method, you are turning an adverse witness into your witness, reminiscent of the scene in the movie *The Verdict*, where Paul Newman's expert witness has just been destroyed by the other side, and Newman turns to his mentor (Jack Warden) and asks "What do you do when you don't have a witness?" Warden replies: "You use their witness."

Constructive cross examination can also take the form of playing one adverse witness against another adverse witness. Assume you are cross examining a witness after several adverse witnesses have already testified. If you can bring out contradictions over the same set of facts by different adverse witnesses, you have obviously succeeded in compromising the opponent's case. Search for information imparted by the witness in direct examination that contradicts other witnesses called by the adverse party. As the witness discusses the fact in detail, the witness simultaneously damages the other witness, often with no recognition that this is happening. You have then effectively turned this seemingly adverse witness into your witness. The apogee of this type of cross examination is when you are able to use a witness called by the adverse party to contradict testimony given by the adverse party.

You can use constructive cross examination effectively when you are cross examining the opposing side's expert witness. For example, in the case of a business appraisal, you can have the adverse expert note acceptance of your client's personal and corporate tax returns and financial statements. You can elicit testimony that reveals that the opposing expert agrees with all or many of the simple parts of your case, which are really not in dispute.

If you are using both types of cross examination with a single witness, it is better to do the constructive phase first, before the destructive phase. The constructive part is enhancing your case, and you want this testimony adduced prior to impeaching the credibility of the witness.

Impeachment by Omission

This method entails locking down the witness' testimony and then demonstrating that what the witness omitted or overlooked is in some manner helpful to your client. For example, suppose in a custody case the forensic expert listed all of the faults he found with the mother as a caregiver. Get a concession that the report covers all of the shortcomings attributable to her that the forensic examiner noted, and then confront the forensic examiner with topics which were omitted and which are subjects favorable to your client.

As another example, suppose an expert's report in a custody case made no mention of the finding of domestic violence perpetrated by the husband. Consider the following series of questions:

Q: Doctor, you issued a report in this case?

Q: A 65-page, single spaced report?

Q: It is a comprehensive report?

Q: You included all of the facts that you considered relevant in your evaluation?

Q: You reviewed the report before you submitted it to the court?

Q: Reviewed it carefully?

Q: Actually, you reviewed it again in preparation for testifying here in court today?

Q: Do you still believe it is comprehensive and states all the relevant facts?

Q: If a spouse has committed domestic violence, would this be a relevant factor in your evaluation? (win, win question)

[If no, pursue]

[If yes] Q: Doctor, please direct the court's attention to the specific page in your report in which you discuss the relevant (looping) factor of domestic violence?

Pure Cross versus Collateral Cross

In a "pure" cross examination, the attorney attacks the substantive testimony of the witness by one or more modes of impeachment, attempting to show that the witness should not be believed and that his opinion or conclusion lacks a proper basis and is in fact erroneous.

Often, and particularly with experts who offer complicated or esoteric testimony, the attorney is not able to substantively confront the witness on his field of expertise, and therefore will not make a direct challenge to the substance of the expert's testimony. Rather, the attorney will use collateral cross examination as an indirect challenge, attempting to demonstrate that for extrinsic reasons, the trier of fact should not trust the testimony. The attorney will often do this by showing bias or interest, as discussed in Chapter 7.

In the case of an expert, a collateral cross examination may entail one or more of the following areas:

- The witness' ongoing relationship with the law firm that is calling the witness as an expert.
- The hired gun approach—the witness relies upon giving expert

testimony as his livelihood and will testify for any side that will pay him.

- Proving that the credentials of the expert are wanting, e.g., a physician who is not board certified; this shows the expert spends all of his time in academia and lacks any practical experience in the field.
- Whether the witness has published any scholarly articles in the field.
- How often the witness has reviewed his report and/or testimony with the opposing side that has retained him.
- Reported decisions which have criticized the expert.
- The amount of the expert's compensation in the case.
- Whether the expert is currently active in the field.
- Consider the following example in the cross examination of a physician:

Doctor, you recall on direct examination, you told the court of your qualifications in the field of psychiatry?

You recall that you told the court that you have testified in numerous courts in New York and in other states as well?

You told the court you have testified over 60 times?

You have been offering expert testimony in your field for 5 years?

So, on average, you testify about 12 times per year?

In addition to testifying, you examine people for the purpose of preparing testimony for litigation?

You charge for your services in and out of court?

A significant portion of your income is related to litigation, for time expended in court and time spent out of court, but related to ongoing litigation?

You intend to continue this aspect of your professional endeavors in the future?

You charge a fee for your daily appearance in court?

Do you differentiate your charge for a half-day as opposed to a full day in court?

How much do you charge for one-half day?

Full day?

Just to examine a patient, is there a set fee or an hourly fee?

[Contrast how much more the witness makes by litigation]

The "Columbo" Cross

Remember Detective Columbo (Peter Falk) of TV fame, with his lazy eye and rumpled raincoat? At first blush he appeared to be a simpleton. Then, he would remark "Just one more question," and you knew he was dumb like a fox. With the right witness, usually an arrogant and pompous one, this approach might work. At first, you appear to be akin to a country bumpkin and lull the witness into a false sense of security, which often leads the witness to overstate her case. Then you hit the witness with the bombshell.

Trick Cross—The Blank "Incriminating" Document

There is an old trial lawyer's trick where during cross examination the lawyer holds in his hand a piece of paper or file and asks the witness if he or she ever put in writing whatever is relevant and incriminating under the circumstances, attempting to induce the witness into believing the incriminating document is in the hand of the lawyer. In reality, the paper is blank or is totally irrelevant to the case. Nowhere was this done more dramatically than by Charles Laughton in the movie, *Witness for the Prosecution*, when in cross examining Marlene Dietrich he holds a paper in his hand and asks her if she wrote a letter to a man named Max. She denies writing such a letter and states that what the attorney has in his hand could not be her letter, as she only writes on short blue stationery. Laughton then lifts from his pile of papers the blue stationery and reads the letter, later confessing to the witness that what he initially held in his hand was a bill from his tailor for a pair of Bermuda shorts.[11]

Combating the "No Basis" Question

There are times when a practitioner on cross examination asks a witness a question that infers the witness committed some heinous or criminal act, although the questioner has no basis in fact to even suggest that such an act was committed. The goal is to raise the specter of the possibility that the witness has acted in an egregious manner, despite any factual foundation for the question.

Such a cross examination is improper and may run afoul of ethical canons and criteria, and court rules of procedure. Specifically, the use of such questions is prohibited by Rule 403 of the Federal Rules of Evidence, which states that "The court may exclude relevant evidence if its probative value is substantially outweighed by the danger of one or more of the following: unfair

---

11. Of course, movie buffs will know that Marlene Dietrich had the last laugh.

prejudice, confusing the issues, misleading the jury, undue delay, wasting time, or needlessly presenting cumulative evidence." In addition, the Model Rules of Professional Conduct Rule 3.4(e) provides that a lawyer shall not "in trial, allude to any matter that the lawyer does not reasonably believe is relevant or that will not be supported by admissible evidence."

9

Verbal Language and Body Language of Cross Examination

Cross examination, like all other aspects of a trial, is to an extent theater. As such, the language you employ—both verbally and bodily—is important.

Language of Cross Examination

While there is no unanimity on all aspects of correct verbal or body language, what follows are some tips and suggestions offered for consideration. With respect to the language of cross examination:

- Avoid opening salutations. As previously noted, avoid these meaningless and unnecessary pleasantries imparted to the witness at the very onset of cross examination. Nobody believes they are sincere in substance, and they violate the rule of primacy.
- Avoid framing questions with negative endings, such as "did you not?" or "have you not?" or "are you not?" They are confusing, they compromise clarity, and they are fraught with danger. If the witness answers "no," it isn't clear whether this is affirmative or negative. Confusion abounds. If you need to use a tagline at the end of a question, use "correct," "true," or "right."
- Avoid pompous vocabulary, particularly with lay witnesses, and wherever possible avoid legalese. Say the parties signed a contract, not

executed a contract. The parties canceled an agreement, not vitiated or abrogated an agreement. The witness was guilty of a wrongdoing, not a transgression.

- Avoid repeating the testimony on direct examination as a preface to a question on cross examination. To do so merely makes the question unduly long and reinforces the direct examination. Similarly, don't start questions with unnecessary phrases like "Let me ask you this question . . ."

- Wherever possible, use memorable words or phrases. In a world of sound bites, we are trained to remember a few memorable words, such as, "Having told us you were drunk at the time," "When you viciously assaulted your spouse," etc.

- Use power language. Use powerful words and phrases to make your point. "You *viciously* struck the plaintiff?" "You acknowledge that you *grossly* understated your income on your 2009 tax return?" Conversely, avoid differential and uncertain words and phrases like "maybe," "possibly," "probably," "I believe," or "I think." They are words of obfuscation and tend to produce an equally bewildering answer.

- In referencing the opposing witness' sworn statements, do not refer to it as "testimony," nor allude to the witness as "testifying." Opposing witnesses "claim," "give their version of the facts," or "tell their stories." Your witnesses "testify," a word cloaked with the aura of truth. Thus, do not start a question on cross examination with "On direct examination, you testified . . ."

- Frame your questions to receive a "yes" answer. Wherever possible, your leading questions should be framed to elicit an answer of "yes" as opposed to "no." Framing the statements you make (declarative questions) in a positive rather than negative manner makes the answer easier to understand. For example:
  - Negative phrasing: "You have not met Mr. Jones before?"
  - Positive phrasing: "This was the first time you met Mr. Jones?"

- Avoid conclusive statements. When you begin your question with a word that connotes you are seeking a conclusion, as opposed to a fact, you invite witness participation—something to be avoided on cross examination, save the monosyllabic answers of "yes" or "no." Questions that begin with "therefore," "so," or "still" are asking for conclusions that cue the witness to opine about the subject, which is the last thing you want to occur on cross examination. You should be asking about facts, not conclusions. If you elicit facts favorable to your case, the conclusions will follow. It is a much easier exercise to have a witness concede a fact rather than a conclusion.

- Use only one fact per question. To follow the mandate of only asking leading questions, the most effective method is to limit a question to one fact. With the proper rapid rhythm of a well-planned cross examination, this will not unduly prolong the cross examination. In fact, it will quicken the pace and total time of cross examination. Weave out extraneous details from the question. If such details are essential, make them into separate questions.

- When necessary, ask questions which lend contextual significance to the question(s) that follow. These are referred to as signposts. For example, if you are cross examining an appraiser of a closely held entity, you might ask him, "Is the capitalization of excess earnings method a generally accepted method of valuing a closely held business?" He should answer "yes," which is the answer you want to elicit because that is the method your expert employed. However, the trier of fact should have the aid of contextual significance to the question. Consider the following:

  - Q: You are aware, Mr. Appraiser, that the business appraiser retained by the defendant in this case valued the defendant's business using the capitalization of excess earnings method?
  - Q: That is an accepted method of valuation of a closely held entity?

Now the trier of fact knows why you elicited this testimony and it doesn't get lost in the mountain of testimony adduced.

- Avoid begging. When not totally satisfied with the answer of the witness, avoid language such as "but you're not absolutely certain" or "you can't be absolutely sure." Use subsequent questions to try to make your point—begging won't do it.
- Know which answers you should not accept. If the witness gives any of the following equivocal responses, don't accept them, and instead proceed to pin the witness down:

  - Answering a question with a question.

    Q: Did you pay the mortgage on the marital residence in July?

    A: Why wouldn't I?

  - Ambiguous words or equivocal words in the answer.

    Q: Please describe the girl you saw?

    A: She was young.

  - Nonverbal responses.

    Q: What did the plaintiff say when you confronted her with the letter?

    A: She went like this [shrugging of shoulders or some other gesticulation].

- Guessing or supposing.

    Q: Did you sign the financial statement?

    A: I'm pretty sure I would have.
- Stating what he or she "normally" does.

    Q: Did you review the tax return before you signed it?

    A: Normally I would.
- Don't let the witness use hedge words. Don't let the witness get away with words like "I believe," "to the best of my recollection," "it appears," "it seems," etc. Press the witness.
- Change your voice inflection. When you have reached the crescendo of the line of questioning, and are eliciting the gravamen of the damaging testimony, change the pace and inflection of your voice. If you normally question in a quiet manner, raise your voice. If you normally question in a louder tone, move closer to the witness and lower your tone. Dramatic effect enhances the impact of the damaging testimony. Avoid a strident tone when the questions are preliminary or soft. Save the modulation and strong rhetoric for the issues in controversy.
- Be patient. Part of a patient cross examination is the ability to recognize that the witness subject to the cross examination will attempt to thwart your goal and will fight you whenever there is an opening to do so. Never show that you are baffled by a witness' response. Don't lose your composure when you receive an unexpected or harmful answer; instead, conceal your disappointment. Just calmly either persist in your questioning along the same line, or switch to another tact as seamlessly as possible.
- Personalize your client. Early in the trial, refer to your client by her first name. In contrast, the opposing party is referred to as the defendant or the plaintiff.

Body Language

The parts of a stage in a theater—down stage, up stage, stage left, stage right—have significance, as does the manner in which the cross examiner uses the courtroom. The examiner's body language, eye contact, expression, demeanor, and physical stance send messages, as do those of an actor. A few suggestions to consider are as follows:

- Enter the witness' personal space. Some cross examiners want to approach the witness and "get in the witness' face," particularly at a propitious moment. Some judges allow this, some don't. The witness' anxiety has to be heightened when the examiner is in his face. The goal is to put the witness in a position where to save face in the court-room, the witness will be more inclined to agree with your leading questions. Remember that while you may want to increase the anxiety of the witness by closing in on him, don't stand directly beside the sitting witness (most judges won't let you do this anyway). If you do, you are now sharing the center stage with the witness.

During the impeachment stage of the cross examination, consider mov-ing closer to the witness to heighten the anxiety and pressure. If you desire to have the witness raise his voice in answer to a particular question, move away from the witness. This will trigger an involuntary reaction for him to raise his voice.

- Know where to stand. As we noted previously, during direct examina-tion, the witness is the star, the center of attention. The lawyer's role is one of a conductor or director. Accordingly, during direct examination, remain as stationary as possible and stay partially hidden behind the podium. During cross examination, however, the examiner, through the skillful use of leading questions, is effectively testifying and rel-egating the witness to the rote role of answering "yes" or "no." To be the star and reside at center stage, the attorney has to leave the lectern (lecterns generally cover two-thirds of your body), become peripatetic, and stand to the side or in front of the lectern. When you watch pro-fessional speakers, and particularly Sunday morning preachers, they move aside from the back of the podium.
- Do not remain stationary. Many witnesses, by habit or instruction, look at the judge while answering a question in an effort to gain cred-ibility by making eye contact with the judge. This can be thwarted by moving from place to place while questioning, so the witness is compelled to follow you and make eye contact with you, not the judge. It also can be thwarted by asking rapid questions that call for "yes" or "no" answers and don't give the witness the time to glance toward the judge.
- Don't question with a pencil or pen in your hand. It is an unnecessary distraction. You want the witness to be watching you, not the pencil.
- Use eye contact. It is crucial for effective communication. Remember the old adage from childhood: "Don't trust someone who you can't look in the eye." Keep your eye contact on the witness at all times. You can't do this if you are a slave to your notes, or glued to an outline or script. Eye contact will enable you to gauge the comfort level of the witness as she answers questions, and often a witness' eyes will send you a signal that you have hit pay dirt in the line of questioning you are pursuing. If the eyes of the witness were upon you during your questioning and then suddenly the witness is looking down or staring from place to place, something of consequence is happening.

- Vary your demeanor based on the type of witness you are cross examining. Heavy handedness is not the tactic when questioning a little old lady or a child.
- When you catch a witness in a damaging lie, don't express glee. Use some other movement or gesticulation to express your disgust. Lower your head and change your voice inflection and facial expression, but don't go overboard.

10

Looping

Looping is a concept advanced by Pozner and Dodd,[12] the purpose of which is to emphasize certain facts. The technique involves establishing a fact favorable to your case and then embodying that fact in the succeeding question or questions. Some examples are:

> Q: You told us that at the time in question the defendant was drunk?
>
> Q: When the defendant was drunk (looped the first answer) he was in the presence of his two children?
>
> Q: When the defendant was drunk he had physical contact with the children?
>
> Q: How long did you observe the drunk defendant having physical contact (looping two answers) with his children?

> Q: You told us that the wife is a good nurturing mother?
>
> Q: As a good nurturing mother, she reads to her children regularly?
>
> Q: As a good nurturing mother, she makes sure they receive proper medical and dental care?
>
> [Repeat with other aspects of child rearing]

12. Larry S. Pozner and Roger J. Dodd, Cross Examination: Science and Techniques (1993).

Double Loop—establish Fact 1, then Fact 2, then loop together in subsequent question or questions

Q You were present when Helen signed the prenuptial agreement?

Q: She was crying at the time?

Q: She was hysterical at the time?

Q: Helen, while crying and hysterical (double loop), signed the prenuptial agreement?

Q: You personally witnessed Helen, while crying and hysterical, sign the prenuptial agreement?

Q: Jim weighs approximately 220 pounds?

Q: Ellen weighs approximately 120 pounds?

Q: You saw 220-pound Jim hit 120-pound Helen?

Q: 220-pound Jim beat 120-pound Helen with his fists, correct?

11

Calling an Adverse Party as a Witness

You may call the adverse party as a witness on your case as part of your cross examination strategy. Generally, the attorney who calls the adverse party as a witness should not be bound by the witness' answers and should be permitted to ask leading questions and cross examine, because the witness is obviously hostile. Federal Rules of Evidence section 611(c)(2) permits leading questions "when a party calls a hostile witness, an adverse party, or a witness identified with an adverse party."

Deciding whether to call the adverse party as your witness involves advance planning and strategic considerations. Be mindful of the fact that when you call the adverse party as your witness, the expectation that you are going to do substantial damage to the witness and her case is extremely high. If you complete such an examination and have barely caused a scar on the witness, you have not remained in neutral territory—you have lost ground.

The decision to call the adverse party can, however, be effective in a number of situations. First, if you sense that the adverse party, usually because he or she is a defendant in the action, is unprepared for testifying at the commencement of the trial, you may want to put that party on the stand. By doing so, you also deprive the defendant of the opportunity to have her own testimony "conform" to that of her witnesses.

Second, for the sake of making an important first impression—in this instance a strongly negative one—you could put the adverse party on the stand and cross examine with several blockbuster points to show how distrustful and dishonest the witness is in fact. By doing this, you are introducing the adverse party to the court on your terms.

Third, you may want to call the adverse party on your case when it is absolutely essential to prove an element of your case. In any event, beware of doing an extended examination. Score some points, make the first impression, and sit down.

Calling an adverse witness on your case unquestionably permits you to ask leading questions. The mode of impeachment available for such a witness, however, is a more difficult question. In some jurisdictions, the extent of impeachment is limited. For example, in *Jordan v. Parrinello*,[13] the New York court held that:

> when an adverse party is called as a witness, it may be assumed that such adverse party is a hostile witness, and, in the discretion of the court, direct examination may assume the nature of cross examination by the use of leading questions. However, a party may not impeach the credibility of a witness whom he calls (see *Becker v. Koch*, 104 N.Y. 394) unless the witness made a contradictory statement either under oath or in writing (see CPLR Rule 4514).

13.   144 A.D.2d 540, 534 N.Y.S.2d 686 (2d Dept. 1988).

12

The Collateral Evidence Rule

The collateral evidence rule is a rule of evidence that limits the ability of the cross examiner to contradict the witness by the introduction of extrinsic evidence. It holds that the party who is cross examining a witness cannot introduce extrinsic documentary evidence or call other witnesses to contradict a witness' answers concerning collateral matters raised solely for the purpose of impeaching that witness' credibility.

This rule is premised on sound policy considerations. If attorneys were allowed to introduce extrinsic evidence which is otherwise inadmissible to contradict each and every answer given by a witness solely for the purpose of impeaching that witness, numerous collateral mini-trials would arise involving the accuracy of each of the witness' answers. The resulting length of the trial would by far outweigh the limited probative value of such evidence.

While the collateral evidence rule is said to rest upon auxiliary policy considerations of preventing undue confusion of issues and unfair surprise by extrinsic testimony, when evidence directly challenges the truth of what a witness has said in matters crucial to or material to the issues on trial, by no process of reason can it be held to be collateral. Stated otherwise, a matter is collateral unless it is relevant to some issue in the case other than credibility or is independently admissible in order to impeach the witness. Thus, where the subject matter bears upon the witness' credibility because it shows that the witness had acted deceitfully on a prior unrelated occasion, it is collateral and, if the witness denies the conduct, the questioner is generally bound by the witness' answer and may not refute it with independent proof.[14] However, the cross examiner does not completely have his hands tied as, for example, a negative response by the witness does not preclude further questioning of the witness on the point.

---

14. *See, e.g.*, Peo. v. Pavao, 59 N.Y.2d 282, 288, 464 N.Y.S.2d 458 [1983].

13

Cross Examination by Bad Acts or Conviction

The proffer of character evidence to raise the inference that a witness has acted consistently with a particular character trait is generally prohibited. However, there are certain exceptions where the issue is the witness' reputation for truth and veracity, as opposed to the character of the witness generally.

Specifically, Federal Rules of Evidence section 608(b) states that

> Except for a criminal conviction under Rule 609, extrinsic evidence is not admissible to prove specific instances of a witness's conduct in order to attack or support the witness's character for truthfulness. But the court may, on cross examination, allow them to be inquired into if they are probative of the character for truthfulness or untruthfulness of: (1) the witness; or (2) another witness whose character the witness being cross examined has testified about.

Accordingly, character evidence to support credibility is only admissible after the witness' character has been attacked. Generally, you may cross examine a witness with respect to specific immoral, vicious, or criminal acts which have a bearing on the witness' credibility.[15] When cross examining a witness on a collateral issue bearing upon his or her the credibility, be cognizant of the aforementioned collateral evidence rule, which interdicts the use of extrinsic evidence in such a situation.

---

15. Badr v. Hogan, 75 N.Y.2d 629, 555 N.Y.S.2d 249 (1990).

An example of the use of bad acts as a basis for cross examination was recently demonstrated in a New York case, *Young v. Lacy*,[16] which involved a personal injury action where the defendant's attorney sought to question the plaintiff about her federal tax returns, which showed she filed as head of household for a number of years when she had been married and living with her husband during that period. The court reasoned that if the plaintiff had improperly filed such returns to receive a tax credit to which she was not entitled, she may have committed tax fraud and thus a classic example was made of bad acts impeachment foundation, as tax fraud has "some tendency to show moral turpitude to be relevant on the credibility issue."[17]

Another exception is cross examination by a criminal conviction, which you may inquire into on cross examination, subject to certain limitations and safeguards contained in Federal Rules of Evidence section 609. Unlike many state rules on the subject, the federal rules provide an effective statute of limitations on the use of a prior conviction for impeachment purposes by providing that after ten years following a person's release from confinement (or from the date of his conviction) the probative value of the conviction with respect to that person's credibility is diminished to a point where it should no longer be admissible. A corollary to this general rule is that generally a party has a right to call a knowledgeable witness to testify that a key opposing witness who gave substantive testimony has a bad reputation in the community for truth and veracity.[18]

---

16. 120 A.D.3d 1561 (2014).
17. Badr v. Hogan, 75 N.Y.2d 629, 555 N.Y.S.2d 249 (1990).
18. *See, generally*, People v. Fernandez, 17 N.Y.3d 70 (2011).

14

The Intractable
Witness

No trial lawyer has escaped the experience of cross examining a witness who just refuses to answer the question posed. By doing so, the witness presents a direct challenge to the control the examiner must have over the witness. To overcome this problem and to be able to reassert control, this chapter offers several suggestions.

First, always maintain eye contact with such a witness. By doing so, you are sending a signal that you are not fooling around, that this is serious business. Anything that heightens the anxiety of the witness can work to your favor.

Second, when the witness fails to answer the question posed, say something akin to one of the following:

> *Sir, my question is slightly different from the one you have chosen to answer.*
>
> *Sorry I confused you, let me try again.*
>
> *Can you try to answer my question?*
>
> *You told us you came here to tell the truth. If the simple truth is "yes," please just tell us "yes."*
>
> *So, the answer is "yes"?*
>
> *I know you wanted to say that sir, but my question is . . .*

Third, after the witness gives an unresponsive answer, repeat the very same question. However, this time, start the question with the witness' name; use a rising inflection of your voice, particularly at the end of the question; and repeat the question very slowly in an emphatic tone which gives emphasis to the fact that the witness is not answering a direct, short, straightforward question. Consider the following example:

> Q: You signed the 2015 income tax returns?
>
> A: He brought some papers home and I signed whatever it was—I don't know.
>
> Q: (Slower, eye contact) Mrs. Smith, you signed the 2015 income tax returns?
>
>
> If you cannot get a direct answer after two attempts, try reverse repetition, as follows:
>
> Q: You are telling this court that you did not sign the 2015 income tax return?

Reverse repetition can be useful in a number of instances. It simply reverses the question.

Consider also this example:

> Q: Did you speak to the defendant again?
>
> A: It was not necessary.
>
> Q: My question is slightly different from the one you have chosen to answer. Did you speak to the defendant again?
>
> A: I told you it was not necessary.
>
> Q: Are you telling this court that you had a second conversation with the defendant?
>
> A: No.
>
> Q: You never spoke to him again?
>
> A: Yes.

There are several things that you should not do, or do only as a last resort, when dealing with the intractable witness. First, do not tell the witness at the onset of cross examination that you can answer only "yes" or "no"; the likelihood is that the court will correct you and you have immediately lost standing with and control of the witness. Additionally, it violates the rule of primacy.

Asking the judge for help, i.e., "Please direct the witness to answer my question with 'yes' or 'no' if possible," is an action of last resort. You appear to be whining. You have just admitted that you have lost control of the witness. Asking for judicial intervention at this stage is additionally problematic because the judge may say to the witness: "Answer 'yes' or 'no' if you can; if you can't, tell the attorney the question cannot be answered 'yes' or 'no.'" The witness has now, with apparent judicial imprimatur, been keyed to means of evading direct answers and concomitantly has been given a license to explain and narrate, by just stating "I can't answer that question 'yes' or 'no.'"

As previously noted, the more experienced trial lawyer will veer from the rules and commandments from time to time. It may, for example, be appropriate when you are cross examining a witness who has shown himself to be both evasive and arrogant to dispense with the leading questions. The full flavor of the evasiveness and arrogance will not be shown by a series of staccato, short questions designed for "yes" or "no" answers. You have to let the witness talk a little to underscore and highlight the full flavor of his obnoxious traits.

15

The "I Don't Remember," "I Don't Know" Witness

The sudden onset of amnesia that disproportionately afflicts people subject to cross examination is well known to trial lawyers and is something you must confront. First, you must make a decision as to whether the witness' inability to remember or know is reasonable and plausible, or patently absurd. If the former, move on, or ask questions that may refresh the witness' recollection. If the latter, pursue.

Don't be discouraged by the inability to recollect. Rather, ride it until it is dry. The more times a witness says "I don't remember" and "I don't recall," when common sense tells us they should remember the answer, the better. Test the witness' inability to recollect. For example, if an amount of money is involved, ask if it is more or less than $1,000, more or less than $5,000, or such other figures as may be appropriate to the question.

Study the witness' direct testimony and her ability to recall dates and places with alacrity, particularly events that long preceded the event you are asking about. Contrast the witness' ample memory of facts that help her case with the dearth of memory of relatively contemporaneous facts that hurt her case.

Drive home the failure of the witness to remember a momentous event in the witness' life or other momentous events about which she clearly should be aware. For example, in one case, the wife was questioned as to when she first contacted a divorce lawyer. The cross examination, edited for brevity, was as follows:

Q: When did you first contact Mr. _____, your matrimonial lawyer?

A: I don't remember.

Q: Can you tell us the year that you contacted him?

A: No.

Q: Can you tell us the month you contacted him?

A: No.

Q: The time of year, spring, summer, fall winter?

A: No.

Q: Mr. _____ was the first matrimonial lawyer you ever contacted?

A: Yes.

Q: You contacted him after you had been married to your husband for over 15 years?

A: Yes.

Q: The decision to contact a matrimonial lawyer was one that you thought about long and hard before doing?

A: Yes.

Q: This was a momentous decision on your part to contact a matrimonial lawyer?

A: Yes.

Q: It was the first and only time in your life that you made an initial contact with a matrimonial lawyer?

A: Yes. (This shows how it is not plausible that the witness would have no recollection of when this event occurred.)

16

Closing Escape Hatches

"Much depends upon the sequence in which one conducts the cross examination of a dishonest witness. You should never hazard the important question until you have laid the foundation for it in such a way that, when confronted with the fact, the witness can neither deny nor explain it." – FRANCIS WELLMAN, THE ART OF CROSS EXAMINATION (1905)

When you are cross examining with a prior inconsistent statement, you must commit the witness to his direct testimony, show the importance and seriousness of the inconsistent statement, and then confront the witness with the inconsistent statement. This way, you will close all the witness' escape hatches before hitting him with the cross examination punch. This method applies to all aspects of cross examination. It is essential that you foreclose the witness from offering any possible explanations before you confront him with the main point or impeaching material.

Suppose you are prepared to launch an attack on the methodology employed by an expert witness in reaching his conclusion. You want the witness to be firmly committed to the methodology employed before you launch the attack. Consider the following:

Q: Doctor, you described the methodology you employed in reaching your conclusion?

Q: You made sure you considered all the relevant facts?

(continued)

Q: Your methodology was complete?

Q: To the extent it was not complete, it would be wrong and less reliable?

Q: Your investigation and methodology was fair?

Q: To the extent it was not fair, it would be inappropriate?

Q: Your methodology was in conformance with standards promulgated in your profession?

Q: You believe you did not overlook any relevant facts?

17

Patience and Pacing

The Necessity for Patience

Part of the discipline necessary to conduct an effective cross examination involves having the requisite patience to develop the cross examination. Patience is a clear virtue in the conducting of a cross examination. We all want to get to the "closer," that moment of great impact when we shatter the witness' veneer of credibility. That will not happen, however, unless we build up to the crucial moment, and that takes patience and discipline. We have discussed closing escape hatches and cross examining with a prior inconsistent statement, all of which takes patience.

As an example, suppose you are cross examining an expert witness who espouses a scientific theory in a particular scientific discipline. You want to bring out that his theory has not been parsed and vetted by the process known as peer review. You could simply ask the witness "Have you ever submitted your opinions for peer review?" With a patient buildup, however, the impact is substantially greater. Consider the following series of questions:

Q: You are familiar with the peer review process?

Q: By peer, we are referring to people in your area of science?

Q: So, the peer review process involves a review of one's opinions by scientific peers or colleagues?

Q: It allows you to get valuable feedback from other scientists about what they think of your opinions?

(continued)

Q: *It provides a sense of whether your opinions are generally regarded as supportable and reliable by other experts in your field?*

Q: *This can be very valuable in the scientific process, correct?*

Q: *One form of peer review involves standing up at meetings and sharing your views with peers of fellow colleagues?*

Q: *And you are discussing the bases of your opinions with them?*

Q: *This allows your peers to comment on the strengths or weaknesses of your opinions?*

Q: *You have been involved in this litigation for four years, correct?*

Q: *You have never stood in front of a group of your fellow scientists to share with them the opinion you shared with this court on direct examination?*

Q: *Another form of peer review is publishing articles?*

Q: *When you submit an article to a professional journal, the article is peer reviewed before it is published?*

Q: *This, too, can be a valuable part of the scientific process?*

Q: *It might help weed out what is generally referred to as "junk science"?*

Q: *You have never submitted a manuscript stating your opinions as expressed to this court today to a journal for publication?*

Pacing

Generally, it is essential that the pace of cross examination, with certain exceptions to be discussed, be fast and crisp. The witness thereby has less time to think between questions and it is easier for the examiner to maintain control. The momentum must be sustained. In football, a "hurry up, no huddle" offensive play is designed to not allow the defense the time to organize and set up. The same principle applies in cross examination. The use of short, leading questions, with one fact per question, quickens the pace of cross examination and affords the witness little, if any, time to mentally develop an escape hatch.

Develop the ability to ask questions that are really not subject to objection. Objections disrupt the pace and cadence of a well-planned cross examination. Realize that opposing lawyers often make objections solely for the purpose of breaking the flow of an effective cross examination. By asking questions which are not objectionable, you will limit the opponent's ability to level objections.

There are some notable exceptions to the rule about a fast, crisp pace for cross examination:

- When you are unloading the key question of impeachment, the big blow, change your pace, slow down, change the tone and inflection of your voice, and enhance the dramatic moment. This is not just another question—this is the pinnacle of your examination and is worthy of special treatment.
- When the witness is squirming, refusing to answer the question, or engaging in pregnant pauses between questions, don't rush anything. Let the visual play out.
- Whenever you want the trier of fact to absorb fully the import of an important question and answer, don't rush the moment—act deliberately.

There are other times when a quieter, slower pace of examination will elicit more favorable responses, particularly with delicate witnesses such as children, elderly witnesses, infirm witnesses, and the like. "The experienced advocate, like the seasoned baseball pitcher, relies on his ability to change the pace to suit the varying conditions in the game."[19]

---

19. Francis X. Busch, Law and Tactics in Jury Trials 533, Vol. 3 (1960).

18

Preparing Your Witness for Cross Examination

While the focus of this book is to aid the cross examination of adverse witnesses, the trial lawyer must also prepare her witnesses for cross examination. This chapter reviews some basic admonitions and instructions for a witness about how to comport herself and testify during cross examination.

Some General Advice

It is important for the witness to understand the following about cross examination:

1. Do not argue with the cross examiner.
2. Only answer the question put to you; do not volunteer additional information.
3. If you do not know the answer, say so. Do not guess.
4. If you do not remember, say so.
5. Above all, listen to the question.

The Usual and Customary Questions

Almost every witness on cross examination is asked a series of questions as follows:

> *Are you here today because you were served with a subpoena to appear in court?*
>
> *Did you meet with Mr. Smith's attorney (the opposing attorney) prior to testifying today?*
>
> *Did you speak with Mr. Smith's attorney prior to testifying today?*
>
> *Did you discuss with Mr. Smith's attorney the subject matter of your direct testimony prior to testifying on direct examination?*
>
> *Did you discuss with the plaintiff the subject matter of your direct testimony prior to testifying on direct examination?*

Experience has shown that for some reason, a number of witnesses tend to be less than truthful (they lie!) when asked if they met with and/or talked to the opposing attorney prior to taking the stand to testify. They apparently believe there is something inherently wrong with doing this when, in fact, there is nothing wrong. As we know, what would be wrong is if the opposing attorney did not speak to a witness she called on her case prior to putting the witness on the stand, save a known hostile witness.

Of course, to properly prepare your own witness for cross examination, explain to the witness that there is nothing wrong with speaking to you and discussing the proposed testimony. In fact, it is a good idea to steal the thunder of cross examination and ask the witness on direct examination something along the lines of the following:

> *Q: Did you meet with me prior to giving your testimony today?*
>
> *A: Yes.*
>
> *Q: How many times did we meet?*
>
> *A: One time.*
>
> *Q: When was that?*
>
> *A: One week ago in your office.*
>
> *Q: Did we discuss the topics and types of questions that I would be asking you?*
>
> *A: Yes, we did.*

> *Q: Did I suggest to you the answers you should give?*
>
> *A: No.*
>
> *Q: Are you here today because you were served with a subpoena to appear?*
>
> *A: No.*
>
> *Q: So you are here voluntarily?*
>
> *A: Yes.*
>
> *Q: Why?*
>
> *A: Mrs. Smith asked me to testify, told me what the subject matter of the testimony would be, and I thought it would be the right thing for me to do, that is to come to court and tell the truth about these issues.*
>
> *Q: How did you come to court today?*
>
> *A: I drove myself from my home to court.*
>
> *Q: Did you drive with anyone?*
>
> *A: No.*

The "Memory Question"

When an attorney cross examines a witness about an inconsistent statement the witness made long before the trial with the testimony the witness gave on direct examination, it is common for the attorney to say to the witness, "You would agree with me that your memory about [the event in question] was better three years ago than it was this morning when you testified?"

Many witnesses, acknowledging the general logic inherent in the question, answer in the affirmative. Discuss with your witness that despite the lapse of time, the question may be properly answered in the negative. For example, the witness may state: "I do not agree with your statement. In recent months, I have reviewed numerous documents about [the event in question] and it has substantially refreshed my recollection to the point where I have a better recollection today than I had three years ago."

Avoiding Exactitudes on Direct

A witness who testifies with exactitude about conversations, events, and particulars can be led into a trap for the unwary. Explain to the witness that if you are asking about a telephone conversation that took place a year ago, you are not expected to recite in haec verba the conversation. The manner in which you frame the question on direct is important. Using the aforementioned telephone conversation as an example, avoid asking the witness "Tell the court what you said to him, and what he said to you." This asks for a degree of exactitude and the witness may be lulled into thinking that such a response is necessary. Rather, consider stating the following to the witness:

> Q: Ms. _____, with respect to the conversation that you just told us took place a year ago, do you presently recall the substance of that conversation?
>
> A: Yes.
>
> Q: Then please tell us in words or substance what was said.

In this manner, the witness has some latitude or wiggle room when questioned about the conversation on cross examination.

Qualifying words like "approximately," "about," or "nearly" accomplish the same objective. The witness is definite enough to tell a credible story, but has not put a straightjacket on herself when it comes to cross examination.

Weaknesses on Direct Examination

While the main function of direct examination is to tell a compelling and credible story which supports your theme of the case, direct examination should also be used to steal the thunder of your opponent on cross examination, where that is possible. Although a particular witness may be necessary for your case, thorough preparation will alert you to the fact that the witness will be hit on cross examination with certain weaknesses and/or inconsistencies. Steal the thunder from your adversary and bring these matters up on direct examination, explaining to the witness in advance the purpose of doing so.

The witness, for example, may answer a question and be asked if she has given a different answer to the same or similar question in the past, and then asked to explain why there was a difference—refreshed memory, review of documents, conversations with others, etc. Although opposing counsel may object on the basis that you are improperly attempting to impeach your own witness, you are really not doing so. You are merely giving the court a complete view of the witness' responses to the same question and explaining any differentiation.

There is no universal agreement as to when during the direct examination you should bring up the witness' potential weaknesses. We suggest that you not do so at the beginning of the witness' testimony—the rule of primacy would come into play and the balance of the witness' testimony may be tainted. Rather, somewhere near the end of the witness' direct testimony may be more appropriate.

Defying the "Yes" or "No" Answer

Many attorneys begin their cross examination by basically instructing the witness to answer "yes" or "no." The follow-up question is then usually "Do you understand that and agree to answer accordingly?" or words to that effect. Counsel the witness to not fall prey to this concession. A fitting answer might take the form of "Counsel, I will attempt to answer each question you pose to the best of my ability, and fully and truthfully. If 'yes' or 'no' fulfills that goal, then fine." Stated otherwise, the witness does not want to concede that each question can be answered with a simple "yes" or "no."

19

Dealing with Objections During Cross Examination

The most effective cross examination is often fast paced and crisp. When your adversary objects to questions you ask, it breaks the flow of the cross examination—the opposing side will often do this just for that purpose. Recognizing the possible objections that your adversary can make will better prepare you to remedy them. A list of basic objections is as follows:

- *Beyond the scope.* The question is beyond the scope of direct examination. Judges differ as to whether and to what extent the cross examiner can delve into matters not covered on direct examination. Federal Rules of Evidence section 611(b) provides that "Cross examination should not go beyond the subject matter of the direct examination and matters affecting the witness's credibility." However, the trial judge has discretion to permit cross examination into new matters "as if on direct examination." Accordingly, the general rule is that you can explore on cross examination any topic brought out in direct examination; you can test the perception, memory, and credibility of the witness; and you can bring out bias or prejudice of the witness.
- *Speculation.* The question calls for the witness to guess or speculate.
- *Argumentative.* This objection, frequently made, is not typically valid during cross examination, because it is, and should be, inherently argumentative. The adversary is really objecting to the cross examiner badgering the witness. The judge has the discretion to determine to what extent the cross examiner can continue to press the witness on a given question or issue.

- *Assumes facts not in evidence.* The question you have asked is predicated on facts which are not in the record.
- *Mischaracterization of the evidence.* The question you have asked is predicated upon a misstatement of a fact or facts in the record.
- *Compound question.* The question is confusing and not capable of a clear answer because it is a compound question, i.e., really two questions compressed into one.
- *Repetitive.* The question has been asked and answered. This is a more valid objection on direct examination. While on cross examination the judge clearly has the discretion to prohibit or limit repetitive questions, he or she will generally grant more latitude in this respect on cross examination.
- *Hearsay.* The question calls for a hearsay answer. For example, "Tell us what your brother said to you about your wife's conduct on June 12." The key to combating a hearsay objection is to focus on two possible responses: (1) that the question does not call for a hearsay answer and state the reason; or (2) that while the question is hearsay, it falls within the penumbra of one of the many hearsay exceptions recognized in the law. For a more detailed discussion, see Chapter 20.
- *Lack of foundation.* This generally refers to the proffer of a document or some other type of evidence to be marked and received in evidence, where the claim is that the proponent of the evidence has failed to properly authenticate the document or other item of evidence. For example, if the cross examiner wants to introduce a photograph in evidence, the basic requirement is that the witness acknowledge that the photograph is a true and accurate picture of the scene sought to be depicted at the relevant time, and that there has been no alteration of the photograph. If you do not lay that foundation, an objection to the photograph is valid. If you have laid the foundation and an objection to admission is made by your adversary, quickly point out to the court that you have satisfied the requirements, await the ruling, and move on.
- *Privileged.* The question calls for an answer which would divulge a privileged conversation. The most common privileges are attorney-client, doctor-patient, and the marital privilege.
- *Relevance.* An attorney can object to a question on cross examination on the basis that the information the question seeks is not relevant or material to the issues in the litigation. Remember that questions which seek to elicit bias, prejudice, or interest of the witness are permissible.
- *Competence.* The witness is not competent to answer the question. The cross examiner would generally make this objection when a lay witness is asked an opinion on an issue, but such an opinion is within the

province of expert testimony, and not within the ken of the ordinary person. There are, of course, opinions which a lay witness can give and which are not within the exclusive purview of expert testimony. Competence also refers to the inability of a witness to testify owing to age, infirmity, or statutory authority. For example, in New York, a husband or wife is not competent to testify against the other in an action founded upon adultery, except to prove the marriage, disprove the adultery, or disprove a defense after evidence has been introduced tending to prove such defense.[20]

To effectively combat objections, be ready to rephrase your question, as frequently that ameliorates any initial criticisms. Accordingly, if the adversary makes an objection and you realize the objectionable nature of your question, do an end run around the objection—withdraw the question and then rephrase. By doing this, you will also minimize the disruption to the quick pace that is crucial in cross examination. Additionally, and particularly with respect to an objection based on relevancy, be prepared to make an offer of proof. If the court initially sustains the objection, ask the court for permission to make an offer of proof. Of course, if that permission is granted, remember that in most instances you will want the witness to leave the courtroom while you make the offer of proof, lest you clue the witness to exactly where you are trying to go with your questions.

When you are combating an objection with reference to applicable statutory or case law, try to avoid the appearance that you are lecturing to an unsophisticated court or a court of limited knowledge. Preface your argument with "As the court well knows, the highest court of this state has held," and phrases of similar import.

---

20. N.Y. CPLR 4502(a).

20

Combating the Hearsay Objection

Hearsay is an oral or written assertion, or non-verbal conduct intended as an assertion, made by a person other than by a witness while testifying, and that is offered in evidence to prove the truth of the matter asserted.

To effectively combat a hearsay exception, you must be able to argue that the question does not call for a hearsay answer, i.e., be prepared to state that the answer would not be hearsay, and the reason therefore. You may also argue that, if hearsay, the question calls for an answer that falls within the penumbra of one of the noted hearsay exceptions, including but not limited to the business record rule, spontaneous declarations, admissions against interest, and party admissions.

Not Hearsay—Not Offered for Truth

Inherent within the definition of hearsay is that when the out-of-court statement is offered not to prove the truth of the facts asserted, but for some other relevant purpose, e.g., to demonstrate the state of mind of the declarant or to demonstrate the state of mind of the person hearing the statement, the hearsay rule is inapplicable and, hence, does not operate to bar the evidence. In short, the statement is then not hearsay. To illustrate this point, assume that the following exchange took place:

> Q: *Did you speak to your sister on June 12?*
>
> A: *Yes.*
>
> Q: *How did you speak to her?*
>
> A: *By telephone from my home phone.*
>
> Q: *What did she tell you?*
>
> A: *She said it was snowing in Colorado.*
>
> Attorney: *Objection, move to strike the answer as hearsay.*

Clearly the statement objected to is an out-of-court statement. The witness is telling us what his sister said. However, the next inquiry is whether the statement is offered to prove the truth of the matter asserted. If it is offered to prove that it was snowing in Colorado on June 12, it is clearly hearsay and the objection should be sustained. However, if the question is asked to prove any other relevant point other than the truth of the statement, it is not hearsay. Suppose, for example, a relevant issue was whether the witness' sister was alive on June 12. The question and answer would be relevant in that the witness spoke to her on that date, and the truth or falsity of the substance of her statement, that it was snowing, is irrelevant. The hearsay rule is inapplicable. Similarly, if it was relevant that the witness' telephone was in working order on the date in question, the hearsay rule would not interdict the question and answer.

Consider an action based a form of marital cruelty. The husband testifies that Joe, a family friend, told him his wife said that he, the husband, was a thief, a scoundrel, and an adulterer. Joe's statement is an out-of-court statement, but the statement is not being offered to prove the truth of the matter asserted (i.e., the husband is not trying to prove he is a thief, a scoundrel, and an adulterer). Rather, the statement is offered just to show that the words were said, regardless of truth or falsity.

State of Mind

Where the mere utterance of a statement, regardless of whether it is true, may circumstantially indicate the state of mind of the hearer or declarant of the statement, and such state of mind is relevant, the statement is not hearsay. In *Khan v. Khan*,[21] the wife, in an action based on cruel and inhu-

---

21.   51 A.D.2d 871, 380 N.Y.S.2d 148 (4th Dept. 1976).

mane treatment, was able to testify to what the husband's paramour stated to her about their adulterous relationship, as the statement was received to prove the wife's state of mind and not for the truth of the statement. Accordingly, when you are confronted with a hearsay objection, consider whether the state of mind of the declarant or the hearer of the statement is in any way relevant, and offer the statement for that non-hearsay purpose.

Verbal Acts

Verbal acts are another type of out-of-court statement that are deemed to be non-hearsay. There are two types: First, verbal acts consist of words that resemble acts in that proof of the mere utterance of the words has independent legal significance. For example, in a defamation action, the witness says, "I heard the defendant state that plaintiff has a loathsome disease." While an out-of-court statement, the mere utterance of the per se slanderous words has legal significance and is exempted from the hearsay rule. In a contract action, an out-of-court statement by a witness that the defendant said "I accept" in response to the plaintiff's offer has independent legal significance; it is the making of the statement itself that is the operative fact. The hearsay rule does not interdict this type of testimony.

Second, verbal acts include words that explain or give unequivocal significance to an otherwise ambiguous transaction. Suppose in a matrimonial action, the wife's parent's payment of the down payment on the couple's marital residence is in issue. Particularly, the issue is whether the funds so advanced were a gift to their daughter alone or to both their daughter and son-in-law. The husband's testimony that his mother-in-law stated at the closing of title that it was her pleasure to make this gift to the two of them lends significance to the ambiguous issue of whether the funds were a gift to his wife alone, or to both of them.

Assume testimony was adduced that money was passed from Person A to Person B and there is an issue as to whether the funds were passed as a gift, a loan, a repayment of a loan, or a bribe. Out-of-court statements can be admitted to explain or clarify the otherwise ambiguous transaction.

To summarize, when the cross examiner is confronted with an objection based on hearsay, the thought process should immediately focus on whether one or more of the following responses are apposite:

- Hearsay is not involved because the question and proposed answer are offered not for the truth of the matter but for some other relevant purpose that you set forth.
- Hearsay is not a valid objection because the question and proposed answer are offered solely to show the state of mind of the declarant or hearer of the statement and such state of mind is relevant.

- Hearsay is inapplicable because a verbal act is being shown.
- Although the question calls for hearsay, it fits within one of the recognized exceptions to the hearsay rule.

As a last resort, when you cannot get by the hearsay objection, ask the witness if she had a conversation with an individual (an out-of-court statement) without relating the substance of the conversation. Then ask the witness "As a result of that conversation, what, if anything, did you do?," which often impliedly relates the import of the inadmissible conversation.

21

Cross Examination of Experts

"An expert is one who knows more and more about less and less." – Nicholas Murray Butler

Don't be afraid to cross examine an expert. While not a facile exercise, you generally do start with a few advantages in cross examining an expert that are not applicable to lay witnesses. Specifically, often the witness steps into the witness box with the aura of "hired gun" attached to her. Experienced judges and lawyers are accustomed to trials by competing hired guns who can take an oath and support almost any proposition.

Second, you generally have had the expert witness' report well in advance of trial, which invaluably facilitates the planning of the cross examination. On occasion, you may have statements of lay witnesses, but not routinely like you will have the reports of experts.

Third, in family law litigation, we deal primarily with experts in the "soft sciences" and professions, as opposed to experts in the "hard sciences," where things can be quantified with precision, measured, and proven by the scientific method. In short, we deal with psychiatrists, economists, or forensic accounting and valuation experts. They employ discretion, judgment, and subjectivity, and dwell in an inexact, empirical world. The psychiatrist who relates clinical judgments, clinical impressions, and hypotheses is dealing in soft science. If the psychiatrist is testifying about the effect of a designated amount of particular drug ingested into one's body, that is hard science. The fact that we confront experts in the soft sciences, with subjective analyses, opens up avenues of cross examination that do not exist as broadly when a conclusion is based on scientific method or theory.

Before we delve into specific methods for cross examining an expert, a few general caveats are discussed.

Type of Cross Examination

You must decide whether to do a direct cross examination, a collateral cross examination, or both. A direct cross examination involves an attack on the substantive findings and methodology of the expert. You are attacking the expert on her own turf and debating her on her area of expertise. This takes extraordinary preparation and skill, and should be planned, where possible, with the aid of an expert in the field who works with you in developing a substantive attack. This is high-risk cross examination, and the need for painstaking preparation cannot be overstated. If you are unable to level the substantive blow, limit yourself to a collateral cross examination where you attack credibility, show bias (testifying for same law firm constantly, funds earned from testifying, etc.), and show inconsistencies in testimony and/or the expert's report. Try to have the witness concede certain facts which are consistent with and possibly bolster the testimony that will be proffered by your expert.

No Necessity for Lengthy Cross Examination

Particularly with an expert, the penchant to cover all aspects of the witness' direct testimony is often a mistake, and serves to buttress the direct testimony by repetition. You are giving the expert another opportunity to build upon her opinion. Rather, choose discrete topics of cross examination for which you are armed with some ammunition. Knowing that you have your own expert to combat the conclusion of the witness, the goal becomes to simply marginalize the expert and punch some holes in her opinion or credibility. In short, you often have to be satisfied with hitting some singles and eschew swinging for the home run.

Complex Financial or Other Testimony

Often, the substance of the expert's testimony can involve rather complex financial or other testimony, e.g., the valuation of a closely held business. If the direct testimony was discombobulated and confusing, you commit a crucial error on cross examination if you clarify and explicate the direct. Do a collateral cross, substantively leave "bad enough alone," and make sure your own expert's opinion is clearly and understandably presented.

When you are cross examining on the complex opinion, remember that it is your task to make sure the trier of fact comprehends the points you are making. Proceed in baby steps. Employ wherever possible the KISS principle: Keep it simple, stupid. Human nature is at work here. We like and adopt what we understand (your case); we avoid and reject what we are incapable of understanding. Ask yourself if you were the trier of fact—if you understood the plaintiff's case but were confused and confounded by what the defendant was trying to prove—where your findings and ruling would most likely fall.

To enhance understanding of your case, if you are cross examining with a deposition transcript, offer the court a copy of the transcript so the court can follow along. If you are cross examining with a spreadsheet, financial statement, or other financial document that has been received in evidence, and the witness has the document before her while testifying, offer the court a courtesy copy of the document to facilitate the understanding of your questioning.

What the Witness Did Not Do

Particularly where your expert has performed a more thorough and comprehensive analysis of the issue subject to expert testimony, it is often effective to cross examine the opposing expert on what she did *not* do. Begin your examination by asking the witness everything she *did* do in order to carry out the specific assignment, be it a business appraisal, forensic child custody analysis, or other issue. Now you have pinned down the witness on what she did, and you can proceed to show what she did *not* do. For example, in a business appraisal situation, the witness may not have made an on-site visit to the business premises; may not have spoken to key personnel of the business; may not have done any industry research; or may not have tested the valuation method with other valuation methods as a so-called sanity check. Where a mental health professional testifies in a custody case, perhaps she did not interview key collateral sources; has never subjected her opinion in this case or other cases to peer review; or did not communicate or with the attorney for the child. The list of items not done could be exhaustive.

Knowing When to Cut Your Losses

You are attempting to score points on your cross examination but to no avail— the expert is doing well. Stop the bleeding, resort to whatever you can gain on a collateral cross, and sit down. You now rely on your expert to carry the day.

The Expert's Report

In almost all jurisdictions, expert testimony must be preceded by a report prepared and filed by the expert. The Federal Rules of Civil Procedure section 26(B)(2), followed by a number of states, provides that the report of an expert witness must contain

(i) a complete statement of all opinions the witness will express and the basis and reasons for them; (ii) the facts or data considered by the witness in forming them; (iii) any exhibits that will be used to summarize or support them; (iv) the witness's qualifications, including a list of all publications authored in the previous 10 years; (v) a list of all other cases in which, during the previous 4 years, the witness testified as an expert at trial or by deposition; and (vi) a statement of the compensation to be paid for the study and testimony in the case.

Once you receive the expert report, preparation demands that you immediately check the credentials of the expert. Where an expert engaged in puffery or misrepresentation regarding qualifications, the entire testimony is tainted.

Second, search for prior testimony of the expert on the same or similar subject matter and see if the subject report is inconsistent with any prior sworn testimony. Similarly, Google the expert and also search by means of LexisNexis, Westlaw, or a similar service. You may find comments and findings about the expert testimony which are critical of the expert and can provide fodder for cross examination.

The expert's report may very well be replete with extrajudicial hearsay statements offered in support of her opinion and conclusion but which are clearly inadmissible under evidentiary standards. In such a case, counsel should consider a pre-trial motion in limine to redact the hearsay statements.

The File of the Expert Witness

At the beginning of cross examination, always ask for the expert's complete file. Many expert witnesses who have testified with frequency learn to selectively bring to court with them the portions of the file that support their opinion, and leave in their office the other portions of the file. Even worse, there are experts who "sanitize" their file before testifying, discarding what they say is not necessary to retain, but which often proves to be material unsupportive of their position. As one noted trial lawyer quipped, "Experts should bring only their laundry tickets to the stand."[22] To combat this, consider serving a subpoena duces tecum on the opposing expert to produce her entire file in court, including, but not limited to, interim report drafts, correspondence with the attorney who retained the expert, notes, memoranda, digital media, etc.

---

22. HENRY G. MILLER, ON TRIAL: LESSONS FROM A LIFETIME IN THE COURTROOM (2001).

Recomputation

An expert may present financial information such as a valuation, income analysis, tax analysis, and so on. Once you have cross examined the witness with contrary proof or other assumptions, and assuming you have been able to get certain concessions from the expert, have the expert recompute the relevant analysis with the proof and concessions you have adduced. For example, if the witness acknowledges that in terms of the value of the subject business, the capitalization rate she employed might be as high as 30 percent, although she used 15 percent in her report, have her do the math while on the stand and inform the court what the valuation would be with the 30 percent capitalization rate.

Using Documents to Refresh Recollection

While this is applicable to all witnesses, expert witnesses in particular often refer to various notes or documents during direct examination to refresh their recollection when asked certain questions. In each instance, the cross examiner should ask the court to have the document so used marked for identification, and the cross examiner should carefully review such documents prior to commencing cross examination. These documents often prove to be gainful fodder for cross examination. Once a witness has used a writing or object to refresh present recollection, the opposing party has the right to inspect it, to use it on cross examination, and to introduce it into evidence.

Reasonable Compensation

In the case of business appraisals, and particularly when the methodology used involves the so-called Formula for Capitalization of Excess Earnings approach to business valuation (see IRS Revenue Ruling 68-609[23]), the issue of reasonable compensation is extant and is an area of common disagreement between competing experts. Reasonable compensation is often referred to as replacement compensation of the individual whose business interest is being evaluated.

Using Databases

Most appraisers use various statistical databases of compensation amounts to formulate the reasonable compensation figure. The cross examiner should thoroughly explore these databases, as there are a number of variables that affect the proper choice of compensation used for reasonable compensation.

---

23. *See* Appendix C.

The cross examiner should check the database used for particularity. Is the survey of the data applicable to the individual in issue in terms of geographic location, age, size of the business, gender, and so on? For example, the compensation of a radiologist in Manhattan clearly differs from that of a radiologist from a small town in the Midwest. In short, the less particularized the information is to the individual in issue, the less reliable is the data used to formulate a reasonable compensation figure.

In addition to a possible attack on the database used, the cross examiner should also confront the witness with the following, if applicable:

- The witness has never had any direct experience in the particular industry being evaluated, and is otherwise unfamiliar with compensation levels.
- The witness has never served in the staffing business or as a headhunter in this or any other industry.
- The witness' basis of compensation is predicated upon one of a number of surveys. To the extent the survey relied upon is incorrect or incomplete, so is the witness' utilization of the survey. Stated otherwise, "garbage in, garbage out."
- The databases themselves contain disclaimers. Look at the disclaimers or statements of limiting conditions often published in the database surveys and confront the witness with these disclaimers.

Being in control is more imperative in the case of an expert witness than a lay witness. You cannot give the expert the opportunity to make speeches. The expert will battle your attempts at control at every opportunity. Be more tenacious than the expert in your quest to maintain control. The use of short, specific, leading questions is crucial. If you ask the expert a generalized question such as "Upon what do you base your opinion?," you might as well plan a strategic exit from the courtroom. Even if you return a half-hour later, the expert will still be explaining. Such a question is a recipe for disaster.

Qualifications of the Expert and Voir Dire

When the opposing expert first takes the stand and your adversary elicits her educational and professional background to qualify her as an expert, you must decide if you will challenge her qualification as an expert. You may challenge whether the expert possesses the requisite skill, training, education, knowledge, or experience necessary to give reliable information and opinions.

In most cases, a challenge will not be advisable and the use of a voir dire to question the witness about her qualifications may only amplify her qualifications. However, there are instances where despite the fact that the proposed expert may possess an impressive academic or professional background, she may not be qualified to opine about the specific issue involved in the case.

Voir dire can be a useful adjunct to the eventual cross examination of the witness. In fact, it can serve as a mini cross examination designed to expose the expert's lack of qualifications in the area she intends to proffer expert testimony. Remember that the voir dire comes right at the beginning of the expert's examination. As a matter of strategy, you may want to show that despite the impressive curriculum vitae of the witness, the witness lacks practical experience in the field, or that the issue in this case is not related or is just remotely related to the subdivision of expertise that the witness has in the field. The fact that someone is a CPA and may be a brilliant tax practitioner does not mean ipso facto that such an individual possesses the requisite credentials to value a closely held business.

In short, where possible, use voir dire to remove any halo that surrounds the witness because of her impressive academic and/or professional curriculum vitae. While you are mindful that the court will, in most instances, not sustain your challenge and will let the witness testify (usually commenting that what you have elicited goes to the weight only of the witness' proposed testimony, not to admissibility), in reality you have a more limited purpose—to show that the doctor is not board certified; that the CPA lacks forensic experience; that the expert has never authored a professional article; that the witness lacks practical training or experience in the field; or that the fact that the witness is a chief of a department means that a great deal of her time is expended in management, labor issues, or fund-raising, and not in academic pursuit. You have thus punched a few holes in the façade of the witness' respectability at the onset of her examination, and have usually increased the anxiety level of the witness—both of which are desired results.

Remember that voir dire offers the cross examiner a unique opportunity, i.e., to question the opposing witness during the course of direct examination. You can use voir dire not only to challenge the credentials of the witness, but to challenge the foundation for the admissibility of various proffers of evidence. Voir dire can help keep evidence out of the direct case and can have the collateral benefit of interrupting the flow of direct examination.

Beware of the expert who exaggerates if not misstates her qualifications. If you are armed with such evidence, consider the following questions to set up the witness with the evidence you have:

> Q: You have stated your qualifications to the court?
>
> Q: They are accurate and complete?
>
> Q: You would not exaggerate or misstate your qualifications, would you?
>
> Q: To do so would be misleading and inappropriate, you agree?

Many experts regale in the numerous professional organizations of which they are members. Familiarize yourself with these organizations. Some require rigorous testing while others require little more than the payment of a membership fee. Consider the following:

> *Q: There is no test taken or required to become a member of that organization?*
>
> *Q: You simply pay a membership fee and annual dues and you are a member?*
>
> *Q: You are aware that Mr. _____, the opposing expert in this case, is board certified in your discipline?*
>
> *Q: To become board certified, you must pass a test and peer review, correct?*
>
> *Q: Is it also correct that you are not board certified?*

The direct examiner will generally elicit testimony from an expert about the expert's past experience in testifying in courts in other jurisdictions on the relevant subject matter. The implication is that other courts have accepted this individual's testimony as expert testimony on numerous occasions and thus some special significance should be attached to what the expert opines. Often, experience in testifying means little more than that giving expert testimony is a significant or sole part of the witness' remuneration.

Consider the following colloquy to challenge a mental health professional who has opined in a child custody case:

> *Q: In reciting your qualifications, doctor, you told us you have testified on numerous occasions?*
>
> *Q: And many of those occasions involved the issue of the determination of child custody, correct?*
>
> *Q: In many of those cases, doctor, and unlike this case, there was no restraint placed upon you in making a recommendation that one parent or the other should be the sole custodian, or that the parents should be joint custodians, true?*
>
> *Q: And there are occasions when you recommended sole custody, and occasions where you recommended joint custody?*

Q: Doctor, after you testify in a case, you leave the courtroom, correct?

Q: You don't stay in the courtroom to hear the rest of the testimony?

Q: In some cases, doctor, do you even know if the court followed the recommendation you made or made some other custodial arrangement inconsistent with your recommendation?

Q: You keep no running record or statistics, do you doctor, about when the court follows your recommendations or does not follow your recommendations?

Q: Doctor, you made recommendations on custody evaluations for a good number of years, am I correct?

Q: So where the court has followed your recommendations, the children subject to these proceedings have grown and presumably matured over the years?

Q: Doctor, have you made any follow-up studies as to how the children have fared over the years, where the court has followed your recommendation?

Q: Conversely, have you made any follow-up studies as to how children have fared over the years when the court has not followed your recommendation?

Q: So, doctor, we have no quantitative or empirical means of testing the validity or efficacy of your recommendations, as we don't know how these children have fared over the years?

Q: Doctor, whether you've testified three times or in excess of 30 times as you stated, we really haven't learned anything from your experience because of the lack of any empirical or other data as to the development of the children?

Professional Standards

Almost every profession has professional standards and guidelines that are promulgated by the particular discipline's professional societies, academies, and academic credential authorities. For example, the American Institute of Certified Public Accountants has *Statement on Standards for Valuation Services*; the American Psychological Association has *Specialty Guidelines for Forensic Psychology*, *Ethical Principles of Psychologists and Code of Conduct*, *Guidelines for*

Psychological Evaluations in Child Protection Matters, and *Specialty Guidelines for Forensic Psychology*; the American Psychiatric Association has a series of guidelines; and the American Academy of Child and Adolescent Psychiatry has *Practice Parameters for Child Custody Evaluation* and *Practice Parameters for Child and Adolescent Forensic Evaluations*.

The Internal Revenue Service publishes guidelines for use by its agents who value closely held businesses. The cross examiner should obtain and study these guidelines and search for places where the witness has veered or deviated from the guidelines.

Search the curriculum vitae and qualifications the expert witness has submitted to the court in order to be declared an expert witness. Often they will reference their membership in these various professional societies and associations, which publish practice parameters, standards, and guidelines. Of course, in the first instance, we must have the witness commit to the guidelines.

Consider the following Q&A:

Q: Doctor, you have been practicing psychology for 20 years now?

Q: During that period of time, you have been a member of the American Psychological Association?

Q: In fact, you have been an active member, serving on various committees of that association?

Q: You are familiar with the fact that the American Psychological Association promulgates guidelines for its members that are engaged in forensic psychology?

Q: As a longtime active member of the American Psychological Association (notice looping), you are familiar with these guidelines?

Q: You have employed these guidelines in your practice?

Q: You have employed these guidelines in connection with the forensic evaluation in this case?

[Develop specific guidelines that have not been followed.]

In an actual case, the husband's witness was a CPA who testified he was an enrolled agent, licensed by the Internal Revenue Service, Office of Professional Management, which means that he was licensed to represent clients before the Internal Revenue Service at any level except the tax court.

He was retained in this case to consult and prepare amended tax returns for the husband, and the manner in which he did this was the subject of the cross examination:

Q: As someone with your vast experience, you are aware that the taxing authorities have promulgated certain standards by which someone like yourself, a tax preparer, must abide, correct?

A: Yes.

Q: That's known as IRS Circular 230?

A: Yes.

Q: And part of IRS Circular 230 says that some like yourself has to perform due diligence in the preparation of income tax returns or amended income tax returns?

A: Yes.

Q: Do you believe you performed due diligence in connection with the subject amended tax returns in this case?

A: I prepared the returns based upon information that the wife's forensic accountant provided in his report.

Q: Sir, the question you answered is slightly different from the one I asked. Did you exercise due diligence as required by IRS Circular 230 in the preparation of the amended returns in this case?

A: Yes.

Q: You are aware that the forensic accountant retained by Mrs. C concluded that Mr. C failed to report over $1,600,000 of income in the four years in question?

A: Yes.

Q: And the amended returns that you prepared for Mr. C now report that income for those four years?

A: Yes.

Q: You made no other changes to the original returns filed other than to include the amount of unreported income for each of the four years in question that totals $1,600,000?

(continued)

A: That is correct.

Q: You know the nature of Mr. C's business, correct?

A: Yes.

Q: You know that it operates as a C corporation, as opposed to an S corporation?

A: Yes.

Q: A C corporation is a separate taxable entity as opposed to a pass-through entity such as an S corporation?

A: Yes.

Q: Did you file amended returns for the C corporation that owns Mr. C's business?

A: No.

Q: You were not requested to by Mr. C or his counsel, correct?

A: That is correct.

Q: When you amend a personal return to include income that was unreported on the corporate return as well, the corporate return should be amended as well?

A: Not necessarily.

Q: Are you telling this court that you can escape corporate tax liability for undeclared income by just amending your personal return and not the corporate return?

A: No.

Q: To abide by established accounting principles, you would have to amend the corporate return as well, correct?

A: If the funds were deposited into the C corporation, yes.

Q: Don't you have to report what should have been reported and deposited into the C corporation, sir?

A: If they are corporate funds. All I had here was a statement saying that the undeclared income was deposited into personal accounts.

Q: As part of your due diligence, you should have attempted to ascertain where the money emanated from?

A: Yes.

Q: Where it should have been deposited, and where it should have been reported on the corporate return?

A: No, I did not do that.

Q: The question was that such an inquiry and finding should have been made as part of the due diligence you told this court you were required to make?

A: Yes.

Q: Did you speak to Mr. C about the undeclared income?

A: Yes.

Q: Did you ask him if there was any further undeclared income that his wife's forensic accountant did not pick up?

A: No.

Q: Do you believe that asking such a question would be part of the due diligence you are required to make?

A: I don't know.

Q: Did Mr. C tell you he agreed with the total number of the undeclared income?

A: He did not state that he necessarily agreed with the numbers.

Q: So you prepared and filed on behalf of a client an amended tax return reflecting previously undeclared income without knowing if the client agreed with the numbers?

A: Yes, I filed it at his request.

Q: Did he quantify to you how he may have disagreed with the amount of undeclared income?

A: No.

Q: Did he tell you that he had more undeclared income than the forensic accountant hired by his wife uncovered?

A: No.

(continued)

> Q: You did no independent audit or check to ascertain if there was any additional undeclared income over and above the $1,600,000?
>
> A: No.
>
> Q: Now, as someone with your vast experience in tax preparation, you must have had the thought, did you not, that you should at least make inquiry as to whether there is any other undeclared income such as cash that was never deposited into the corporation and never reported as gross receipts?
>
> A: Yes.
>
> Q: Did you make any inquiry of Mr. C as to whether he had any additional cash unreported income?
>
> A: No.
>
> Q: Are you telling this court that such an inquiry would not be part of the due diligence you are required to make?
>
> A: No. I was requested to prepare returns based on the forensic audit that had been prepared and that is what I did.

It is fairly common for a spouse in a matrimonial action to have her or his accountant testify about the client's financial condition, with reference being made to personal and business tax returns prepared by the accountant-witness. If the witness is subject to Treasury Department Circular No. 230 (Regulations Governing the Practice of Attorneys, Certified Public Accountants, Enrolled Agents, Enrolled Actuaries, Enrolled Retirement Plan Agents and Appraisers before the Internal Revenue Service), the cross examiner should test her or him regarding the requirements contained in Circular No. 230. Some useful examples are:

- A practitioner must exercise due diligence in preparing or assisting in the preparation of, approving, and filing tax returns, documents, affidavits, and other papers relating to Internal Revenue Service matters.[24]
- A practitioner may not advise a client to take a position on a document, affidavit, or other papers submitted to the Internal Revenue Service unless the position is not frivolous.[25]

---

24. Treasury Department Circular No. 230 §10.22
25. *Id.* §10.34 (a)(1)

- A practitioner may not advise a client to submit a document, affidavit, or other paper to the Internal Revenue Service that contains or omits information in a manner that demonstrates an intentional disregard of a rule or regulation unless the practitioner also advises the client to submit a document that evidences a good faith challenge to the rule or regulation.[26]
- A practitioner advising a client to take a position on a tax return, document, affidavit, or other papers submitted to the Internal Revenue Service, or preparing or signing a tax return as a preparer, generally may rely in good faith without verification upon information furnished by the client. The practitioner may not, however, ignore the implications of information furnished to, or actually known by, the practitioner, and must make reasonable inquiries if the information that is furnished appears to be incorrect, inconsistent with an important fact or another factual assumption, or incomplete.[27]

Jack of All Trades Expert

In some instances, the expert being cross examined professes to be an expert on numerous types of assets and/or issues. Endemic in matrimonial litigation is the expert who values all and any types of business assets and other marital assets. A cross examination can be developed to paint the expert as the jack of all trades, master of none, and a professional witness. Consider the following:

> Q: Mr. Pencil, you are a CPA?
>
> Q: You make your living doing forensic evaluations?
>
> Q: You do evaluations of businesses?
>
> Q You also do evaluations of intangible assets?
>
> Q: Like intellectual property?
>
> Q: That includes patents, trademarks, copyrights, and the like?
>
> Q: With respect to businesses, there are many types of businesses, correct?

(continued)

---

26. *Id.* §10.34((b)(2)(iii)
27. *Id.* §10.34 (d)

Q: There are retail businesses?

Q: There are manufacturing businesses?

Q: There are service businesses?

Q: You told us about your training in forensic accounting and business valuations?

Q: This is a complex field?

Q: No two businesses are exactly alike?

Q: No two industries are exactly alike?

Q: There are facts and nuances endemic to each business and industry?

Q: There are experts whose field of expertise is a single type of business or industry?

Q: For example, there are experts that only value car dealerships?

Q: There are experts who only value patents?

Q: There are experts who only value certain types of retail businesses?

Q: Like apparel companies?

Q: There are experts who only value law practices?

Q: Dental practices?

Q: Medical practices?

Q: You are familiar with what is known as SIC Codes?

Q: SIC stands for Standard Industrial Classification, a system devised by the U.S. government to classify industries by four-digit codes?

Q: And these codes appear on corporate and other business tax returns, correct?

Q: There are hundreds of codes, representing hundreds of different industries?

Q: If you and your firm were retained by any company within these hundreds of different industries to value the company, you would not hesitate to undertake the engagement?

> *Q: You value all and any of the business types and industry types that I have mentioned?*

Professional Witness

When you are cross examining a professional witness, as opposed to the expert who testifies occasionally, go at it full speed. Through discovery, obtain documents relative to fee arrangements and billing. Explore the duration and extent of the witness' testimony for clients of the same law firm. Ask about the total compensation she has received from testifying, including the hourly rates, the amount billed, and the amounts paid. If there is a substantial balance due to the expert, ask if it is contingent on her testimony (she will undoubtedly say no, but you have raised the prospect that if she wants to get paid, she should try to keep her client happy).

Suppose you have a university professor who supplements her income with frequent appearances as an expert witness. You have fully explored the amount of revenue from this case and from testifying in general, and the relationship between the witness and the opposing law firm. You can also question as follows:

> *Q: So, it is clear that you make a lot more money doing this consulting and testifying work then you make as a professor back at your university, true?*
>
> *Q: You told us on direct that you have actually testified in court about 20 times in the last several years?*
>
> *Q: For these 20 times, you prepared a report?*
>
> *Q: You did this impartially?*
>
> *Q: Just like you would at the university, correct?*
>
> *Q: In each instance you studied the matter independently and you reached a conclusion?*
>
> *Q: Your conclusion in each case was that the party that was paying you was correct?*
>
> *Q: In not one of those cases did your report support the position of the party in the litigation that was not paying you?*
>
> *Q: Then I won't take another minute of your time.*

Another tactic would be to reserve your question about the witness' fee until the end of your cross examination, and curtly ask the following:

> *Q: Dr. Jones, you are getting paid $500 per hour to testify here today?*
>
> *A: Yes.*

We all know that the experts who rely on litigation retention for a living aggressively advertise their services. Let the trier of fact know.

> *Q: Incidentally, your firm does a good deal of advertising?*
>
> *Q: You advertise in legal publications, bar association newspapers, and professional journals?*
>
> *Q: You advertise that you specialize in forensic accounting for litigation purposes?*
>
> *Q: You advertise that you are available to testify in contested litigations?*
>
> *Q: Matrimonial cases?*
>
> *Q: Commercial cases?*
>
> *Q: Wrongful death and personal injury cases?*

Cross Examination by Treatise

Cross examination by learned treatise is a special mode of impeachment, reserved for expert witnesses. Generally, the court will exclude scientific books or reports from evidence as hearsay when offered as proof of the facts asserted in them. However, on cross examination, the examiner may confront an expert, for impeachment purposes, with a passage from a treatise or book of recognized authority which is at variance or in conflict with the opinions expressed by the witness. The witness does not need to have read the book or article about which he is being questioned. However, in order to lay the proper foundation for the use of such material on cross examination, the witness must concede its authoritativeness.

The Federal Rules of Evidence provide that such statements are not excluded by the rule against hearsay:

> Rule 803: (18) **Statements in Learned Treatises, Periodicals, or Pamphlets.** A statement contained in a treatise, periodical, or pamphlet if:

(a) the statement is called to the attention of an expert on cross examination or relied on by the expert on direct examination; and

(b) the publication is established as a reliable authority by the experts admission or testimony, by another expert's testimony, or by judicial notice.

If admitted, the statement may be read into evidence but not received as an exhibit.

When you are employing this mode of impeachment, you must lay the proper foundation for the use of the learned treatise, particularly with the experienced expert witness who knows that she is insulated from such an attack unless she makes certain concessions. Basically, to use a learned treatise to cross examine an expert witness, you must lay one of two following foundations:

1. Show that the witness consulted the particular treatise or relied upon the particular treatise in preparing to testify. An expert cannot avoid cross examination with a treatise if she has already relied upon the text and testified that she agreed with "much of" the book.

2. The witness concedes that the particular treatise is deemed authoritative within the expert's profession. The designation of "authoritative" can encompass a witness' concession that the article is "well-respected," "very competent," and words of similar import.

In one New York case, the court noted that a physician may "not foreclose full cross examination by the semantic trick of answering that he did not find the work 'authoritative' where he has already relied upon the text and testified that he 'agreed with much of it.'"[28]

A sample cross examination on this issue follows:

---

28. Spiegel v. Levy, 201 A.D.2d 378, 607 N.Y.S.2d 344 (1st Dept.1994), *lv. denied* 83 N.Y.2d 758, 615 N.Y.S.2d 875 (1994).

> Q: Sir, you related to us your credentials on direct examination, correct?
>
> Q: As part of your credentials you noted that you are an adjunct professor at Rockland Community College, where you teach forensic accounting and business valuation?
>
> Q: You have taught this course for a number of years, correct?
>
> Q: In teaching these courses, do you assign certain textbooks as part of your course curriculum?
>
> Q: You also maintain certain textbooks relative to these areas of expertise in your private office?
>
> Q: And you subscribe to updates for these texts, correct?
>
> Q: These texts are well-known in your profession?
>
> Q: They are recognized as authoritative in the profession?
>
> Q: You agree with me, sir, that one of these well-known texts in the area of your expertise is Shannon Pratt's text entitled Valuing a Business, 5th Edition?
>
> Q: You assign this book to your students and use it as a text book for your class, correct?

If it appears that the witness will refuse to admit that any writing is an authority, you can challenge her. If she has quoted a text in her expert report, this is evidence that she relied upon the text and thus lays a foundation. You can add to that by asking the witness, "You would not rely upon a text in your report that you did not regard as an authority in the field?"

There is an old trial lawyer's trick where the cross examiner puts three texts on the counsel table and as he holds up each one and questions the witness, the witness flatly denies that the text is authoritative. Then the examiner, in apparent frustration, asks the witness if there is any book or treatise that she regards as authoritative. When the witness announces the name of the text, the examiner reaches down and pulls out the text from the litigation bag and continues the examination.

Although you may use the learned treatise for impeachment purposes, statements in such treatises, even if considered authoritative, are generally not admissible in evidence as proof of the facts or opinions contained therein.

Hypothetical Questions on Cross Examination

Impeachment through the use of hypothetical questions is an additional mode of impeachment you can use, particularly with respect to expert witnesses. In terms of methodology, you would confront the witness with facts that have been developed at trial and tells the witness that she is to assume that the court has heard the testimony and/or received in evidence such facts. You then explore the effect of those facts upon the opinion and conclusion of the expert. By doing so, you are relying on the strength of the opposing evidence, which forms the basis of the hypothetical question, rather than a detailed exploration of the stated opinion. The goal is to use a hypothetical question to weaken the credibility of the witness, turn the witness into your witness, or to show that the expert's opinion does not have a proper basis.

In framing the hypothetical question, you do not need to quote the prior testimony verbatim. You just need to ensure that the hypothetical question contains facts that are "fairly inferable" from the record.[29] Consider the following example, where an expert is being cross examined with respect to a party's enhanced earning capacity:

Q: Sir, in rendering your opinion, you assume certain facts to be true, correct?

Q: One of the facts that you used in making your projection of my client's enhanced earning capacity was the discount rate?

Q: You used a 3 percent discount rate, correct?

Q: You also assume that my client had a work life expectancy of 28 years from the date of valuation?

Q: Sir, I want you to assume that this court has heard testimony that the proper discount rate for this analysis is 6 percent. I also want you to assume that this court has heard testimony that the work life expectancy of my client is 24 years and not 28 years. Assuming these facts to be true, would you tell us what is your opinion of the enhanced earning capacity of Mr. Jones?

Accordingly, where the direct examination does not properly develop the basis and data upon which the expert's opinion is predicated, the cross examiner can use hypothetical questions to challenge the basis. However, the

---

29. *See, e.g.,* Tarlowe v. Metropolitan Ski Slopes, Inc., 28 N.Y.2d 410, 332 N.Y.S.2d 665 (1971).

cross examiner should be mindful that when he or she uses the hypothetical question, it is still the opponent's burden to present a proper basis for the expert's opinion. An expert's opinion testimony must be based on facts in record or personally known to the witness; an expert may not reach a conclusion by assuming material facts not supported by the evidence, and may not guess or speculate in drawing a conclusion.

Attacking the Expert's Report

It is well known that judges generally like to receive the expert's report in evidence, as it can provide an aid to the court. Assuming the expert's report is admitted, you may make a discrete collateral attack upon the preparation of the report itself, as follows:

- Explore who actually wrote the report. Often it is not the expert who is testifying. An associate or junior staff member may have actually written all or a significant part of the report, and that individual is not testifying. This aids an argument about admissibility as well as the credibility of the report.
- Explore who did the leg work and the analysis. The expert testifying may have written or signed off on the report, but was in fact merely adopting the work product and substantive analysis of an associate or junior staff member.
- Explore if the expert independently verified any of the key performance indicators underlying the report, e.g., her valuation conclusion.
- Explore if a draft of the report was sent to the opposing attorney prior to the final report being prepared, and explore the changes from the draft to the final report. As we previously noted, use a subpoena duces tecum to have the witness bring her entire file, including drafts, to court.
- Carefully check the expert's report, upon receipt, for inadmissible hearsay. Although generally you will be provided with expert reports prior to trial, too often attorneys neglect to scrutinize the report. You may uncover clearly inadmissible hearsay and will be able make a corrective motion to strike such material from the report. The fact that an expert can issue a pre-trial report does not afford the expert the license to use an improper basis for her conclusion (see the next section) or to otherwise infuse the report with inadmissible hearsay.

Bases of Expert Testimony

No one should cross examine an expert without first knowing the proper bases of cross examination and vetting the direct testimony to verify if a proper basis has been provided. Remember that expert opinions which are contingent, speculative, or merely possible lack probative force and are, therefore, inadmissible. An expert may neither guess nor speculate. The cross examiner must check if the direct testimony established one of three permissible bases:

1. Personal knowledge of the witness. The witness is, for example, the treating physician or the comptroller of the subject corporation and is testifying from personal knowledge.
2. Facts in the record. A second permissible basis is facts in the record. An expert can testify that she has read the transcripts of the testimony in the record as well as the exhibits received in evidence, and based upon those facts, the expert can offer an opinion. Another way to establish this basis is by posing a hypothetical question in which you ask the witness to assume that the court has heard the following testimony and received the following exhibits, and based upon the facts of the testimony and exhibits, the witness proffers an opinion. In addition to the two methods just mentioned, some courts permit the competing experts to sit at counsel table throughout the trial to assist the trial lawyer, so that the expert is directly cognizant of the facts in the record.
3. Professionally reliable hearsay. This is a third, but partial, basis for an expert opinion. It means that an expert may rely, in part, on out-of-court (i.e., hearsay) material if the material relied upon is deemed reliable within the relevant profession. For example, a vocational expert may rely upon the data presented by the U.S. Department of Labor.[30] A pension actuary may rely upon the benefits booklet published by the union to which the pensioner belongs.

Federal Rules of Evidence section 703, entitled "Bases of an Expert's Opinion Testimony," provides:

> An expert may base an opinion on facts or data in the case that the expert has been made aware of or personally observed. If experts in the particular field would reasonably rely on those kinds of facts or data in forming an opinion on the subject, they need not be admissible for the opinion to be admitted. But if the facts or data would otherwise be inadmissible, the proponent of the opinion may disclose them to the jury only if their probative value in helping the jury evaluate the opinion substantially outweighs their prejudicial effect.

---

30. U.S. Department of Labor, Dictionary of Occupational Titles, 4th Ed. (1991).

If you believe that the expert has not established an adequate basis for her opinion, whether at the end of direct examination or as the result of your cross examination, you should make a motion to the court to strike the opinion testimony of the witness on the grounds that none of the established bases for an expert opinion has been demonstrated.

Collateral Sources

Expert testimony and reports often rely upon third party or collateral sources. This is particularly true in cases involving child custody and access. The cross examiner must be vigilant in ascertaining if a proper evidentiary basis exists for the use of the collateral sources, and should focus his or her cross examination upon that issue. If there is not a proper evidentiary basis, the court should strike the opinion. Often this involves argument about the professionally reliable hearsay rule mentioned in the previous section, and particularly whether "experts in the particular field would reasonably rely on those kinds of facts or data in forming an opinion on the subject" as stated in Federal Rules of Evidence section 703. Remember that the test is whether experts in that particular field reasonably rely upon such facts or data, and not whether this particular witness on the stand reasonably relies upon such facts or data in formulating her expert opinion.

Cross Examination by Disclaimers

Almost all expert reports contain a section which generally is referred to as a "Statement of Limiting Conditions," a euphemistic label for what in reality is a group of disclaimers designed to protect the expert. In effect, the expert is attempting to cover herself from criticism or liability by stating directly what are basically shortcomings in the evaluation process. As such, these disclaimers provide a fertile field of cross examination.

Consider some of these disclaimers, taken from an actual appraisal report:

> We have based our valuation on figures presented by management without a certified statement, nor have we performed an audit of the figures. We have assumed for the purpose of this appraisal that the figures provided by management are correct.

By no means are the disclaimers limited to financial expert reports. They are prevalent in real estate appraisal reports and even in mental health forensic reports. The cross examiner should not only check the expert's report for disclaimers, but also the source material relied upon by the expert. For example, the standard classification and system of nomenclature for psychiatric disorders is the *Diagnostic and Statistical Manual of Mental Disorders*, 5th Edition (DSM-5). The DSM contains the following caveat about forensic use:

> However, the use of DSM-5 should be informed by an awareness of the risks and limitations of its use in forensic settings. When DSM-5 categories, criteria, and textual descriptions are employed for forensic purposes, there is a risk that diagnostic information will be misused or misunderstood. These dangers arise because of the imperfect fit between the questions of ultimate concern to the law and the information contained in a clinical diagnosis.

A cross examination should proceed along the lines of any testimony that has been received which refutes the accuracy of the figures "presented by management" and how that would affect the expert's opinion. The guiding principle is that if the expert relied upon faulty data, the opinion is faulty— garbage in, garbage out.

Here is a similar common statement:

> [ABC Appraisal Co.] will not express any form of assurance on the likelihood of achieving the forecast/ projection or on the reasonableness of the used assumptions, representations, and conclusions.

For a statement like this one, consider a cross examination which emphasizes, for example, the fact that if the appraiser will not vouch for the reasonableness of the assumptions she has utilized, she cannot expect the court to do so.

> We have not conducted a review to determine if significant claims or other contingent liabilities existed as of the valuation date, or currently exist that would impact on the valuation of the subject entity.

If applicable, cross examine the witness about a pending tax audit and/ or assessment against the business, or an environmental issue with respect to the property the business owns and its impact upon the future earnings and prospects of the business.

Cross Examination by the Voluminous Record Rule

The voluminous record rule is a manner of presenting evidence that should be used on both direct and cross examination to cogently and convincingly demonstrate numerous figures or other records. The purpose of this rule is to employ what we previously noted is a basic tenet of human nature—that we tend to agree with things we understand as opposed to things that confound us. There are many examples of when you can use this rule.

Suppose you want to introduce into evidence ten years of tax returns in order to demonstrate some decided trend. Assuming you lay the proper foundation, you can have all ten tax returns received in evidence. Alternatively, you can prepare a one- or two-page spreadsheet of the 1040 form that summarizes the entries on the 1040 form and introduce it as a summary document based on the voluminous record rule. Now you can clearly show any decided trend through the spreadsheet.

From an evidentiary point of view, there are several requirements for the use of the voluminous record rule, which is nothing more than an exception to the best evidence rule.

- The writings or records must be voluminous.
- The originals must be admissible by themselves for the summaries based upon the originals to be admissible.
- There must be a proper authentication of the voluminous records and summaries.
- The originals or duplicates of the voluminous records, while they do not have to be introduced into evidence, must be made available to the opposing side for examination or copying if desired.

Suppose you are cross examining a husband/breadwinner and you are attempting to show that the parties' pre-separation standard of living was in excess of what the husband claims. You have prepared in advance a summary document which charts all of the parties' canceled checks and credit card statements for a relevant period of time, with proper categorization. You confront the witness with the summary document, having laid the proper foundation. You have just made it difficult for the witness to gainsay what you are proving and you have proven the point in a convincing and efficient manner.

In an enforcement proceeding, where a party has accumulated arrears over a protracted period of time, a chart with columns noting date of payment, amount of payment, deficiency in amount of payment per order of the court, and then the total of the arrears can clearly and quickly prove the amount of the arrears. This would replace a tedious process of verbal testimony as to each payment due date and what was paid on such date.

Cross Examination in Child Custody Cases

Tarasoff Cross Examination

In 1976, the Supreme Court of California decided the case of *Tarasoff v. Regents of the University of California*,[31] holding that mental health professionals have a duty to protect individuals who are being threatened with bodily harm by a patient. In that case, the American Psychiatric Association (APA) filed an amicus brief in which they took the position that a mental health professional is not capable of predicting a patient's potential dangerousness. You can use this position of the APA in situations in which a mental health professional opines about future conduct of a parent. An example, taken from the facts of an actual case, and dealing with the issue of a recovering alcoholic parent and whether or not the parent would relapse, is set forth next.

Q: Doctor, your report notes that "the mother describes herself as a recovering alcoholic" and you quote her as saying: "I have been in recovery for 5 or 6 years with one relapse. I have been clean and sober for 3 years."

A: Correct.

Q: You have concluded that the mother's alcohol history does not seem pertinent in making a custody decision?

A: I have so concluded.

Q: So you are stating to this court that in making its decision, this is not a relevant or pertinent consideration?

A: I believe she has made a successful recovery and thus this issue should not be determinative.

Q: Doctor, I didn't ask you if it was determinative. I asked if her history of alcoholism is a relevant and pertinent consideration for the court?

A: I don't believe it is particularly relevant.

Q: Particularly relevant, does that mean it is relevant to some degree?

A: I believe I have stated what I mean.

(continued)

31. 17 Cal.3d 425, 551 P.2d 334.

Q: On page 4 of your report, you note that she is between AA sponsors because of previous sponsor relapse, correct?

A: Yes.

Q: So the person who is assisting her as a sponsor has relapsed?

A: Yes, that is what she told me.

Q: Her father was an alcoholic for most of her childhood, as you note on page 6 of your report?

A: Yes, that is what she related.

Q: A maternal aunt was an alcoholic?

A: Yes.

Q: Her father's male cousin is an alcoholic and former cocaine user who is in recovery?

A: Yes, again that is what she related to me.

Q: The husband reported to you that after the death of her father, she and her mother began drinking, and her mother would bring jugs of wine to the home?

A: That is what he related to me.

Q: Did you check this out factually in any manner?

A: No.

Q: You have not reported that the husband lied to you with this allegation, correct?

A: That is so.

Q: On page 28 of your report, you state: "Husband reports that she once got into a car accident while driving the two boys. She fled the scene with the two children which led to her arrest. I got her out of jail in June of 2002. Two weeks later she was reprimanded by the Committee on Physicians Health because the chairman of her department found her visibly intoxicated."

A: I am stating in my report what the husband alleged, correct.

Q: That is a very serious allegation, is it not?

A: Yes, very serious.

Q: If true, the two boys were placed in a potentially very dangerous situation?

A: Yes.

Q: Did you do anything to validate or corroborate this factual allegation?

A: Not really.

Q: Did you then accept it as true?

A: Yes.

Q: The father reported to you that she had been writing herself prescriptions for Toradol and Percocet, and that she popped Percocet like candy?

A: He so reported.

Q: Doctor, I am correct that you made no efforts to validate, corroborate, or refute this information imparted to you by the father?

A: Other than my conversations with the parties, no.

Q: Did you specifically ask the mother if she denied these allegations made by the father?

A: No.

Q: In contrast, with respect to the father, you note "there is no family history of psychiatric illness, alcoholism, or substance abuse," correct?

Q: Doctor, you're aware that in 2005 the mother suffered a relapse and had to leave the marital home and went to the Betty Ford clinic for rehab?

Q: Doctor, you cannot sit here and tell this court with any degree of medical certainty that she will, as her immediate past sponsor has done, not suffer a relapse again?

A: No, that is not possible to state, although I do not think it would occur.

(continued)

Q: And, as contained in your report, the mother often drives the children to the various extracurricular and other activities?

A: Yes.

Q: And you can't predict with any degree of certainty that if she relapses she will not be driving a car with the children in the car?

A: No.

Q: You're aware that she had a previous DWI?

Q: You're aware that psychiatrists are ill-equipped to predict future dangerous behavior of people they examine or treat?

Q: In fact, doctor, in your training I assume you are aware of the famous court case by the name of Tarasoff v. The Regents of the University of California.

A: Yes, I am aware of that case.

Q: In that case, a young woman student was killed by a student who told a counselor he was seeing at the university that he intended to kill her. The therapist called the campus police, who felt the student appeared rational and no further action was taken. The young woman's parents sued the university because no one had warned the victim, alleging that the therapist had a duty to warn. Those are the basic facts, correct?

A: I am not aware specifically but that sounds correct.

Q: You are a member of the American Psychiatric Association, correct?

A: Yes.

Q: You are aware that the APA filed a brief stating that the duty to warn imposes an impossible burden on the practice of psychotherapy? "It requires the psychotherapist to perform a function which study after study has shown he is ill-equipped to undertake, namely, the prediction of his patient's potential dangerousness."

A: I am aware of that position.

> Q: So, applying that principle to this case, doctor, you cannot tell this court if she will relapse again and if so, whether there'll be danger to the children as a result of the relapse?
>
> A: That is true.
>
> Q: You agree with me, doctor, that a prime function of parents is to provide for the safety of their children?
>
> A: Of course.
>
> Q: Certainly, the physical safety is of the utmost concern?
>
> A: Yes.

Clinical Examination and the Effect of Examiner

In any case involving child custody and access, where there is a forensic evaluation, the cross examiner can call into question the very nature of the clinical examination and circumstances surrounding the forensic examination. Consider the following:

> Q: Doctor, you had multiple examinations of the parents and the children, correct? [recount visits and clinical examinations]
>
> Q: When you did this, doctor, did you have any doubt in your mind that the children knew the purpose for which they were coming to your office?
>
> Q: They knew that their parents were embroiled in a divorce action, which included the issue of which parent they would live with when the action was completed?
>
> Q: Would you state that both the parents and the children, when they met with you, were under a certain amount of stress and anxiety because of the circumstances surrounding their visits with you?
>
> Q: Doctor, is there a very substantial body of scientific and professional literature indicating that the general circumstances under which a forensic examination is conducted (the time, the place, the purpose) affects the kind of information or data that emerges in the examination?

(continued)

Q: Doctor, isn't there research showing that such factors affect the kind of information that is obtained in the interview?

Q: Isn't there described in the literature something known as situation effects?

Q: The pendency of a divorce and custody case could qualify as such a situational effect, correct?

Q: In fact, the DSM describes marital breakup as a psychosocial problem that can affect diagnosis and prognosis?

Q: The breakup of a marriage, particularly when children are involved, is a highly stressful situation. Most normal people, both parents and children, feel and exhibit this stress?

Q: And the behavior observed under the circumstances may not be representative of the individual's behavior under more normal, less highly stressful circumstances, true?

Q: Not only do we have the strain circumstances relating to the divorce and the issue of custody, but the additional strain circumstance of the clinical examination itself?

Q: Doctor, in addition to the psychological stress of a divorce and custody proceeding, is not a fact that a clinical examination is also affected by the nature of the examiner himself or herself?

Q: The attitudes of the examiner, the personality of the examiner, the race or economic status of the subject and the examiner, all have an effect, correct?

Q: You have learned in your studies, doctor, have you not, that some examiners with one theoretical orientation might get different data, and record and interpret the data differently, than an examiner of a different theoretical orientation, correct?

Q: Similarly, examiners with different personalities might get some different kinds of information from the people they examine, true?

Q: That is because people respond differently to different types of people, true?

Q: What the examiner perceives, remembers, and records is also subject to influence, distortion, or bias due to the theoretical orientation of the examiner, the values and attitudes of the examiner, and other characteristics of the examiner?

Q: The interpretation of the data collected is subject to influence, distortion, and bias due to the same factors, am I correct?

Q: In addition, forensic evaluation cases like this necessarily involve a prediction?

Q: And doctor, isn't it a fact that a prediction in this field is overwhelmingly speculative?

Q: And one examiner or clinician can base his/her conclusions on invalidated and speculative theories of child development that differ from another examiner or clinician?

Q: There are different and competing theories of child development?

Q: And doctor, what you have provided us with on your direct examination is what could be called a clinical judgment, is that not correct?

Q: Isn't there a substantial body of scientific and professional literature indicating that there are a number of serious flaws and problems with clinical judgment (i.e., that it lacks validity or cannot be relied upon)?

Confirmatory Bias and the Principle of Primacy

Q: Doctor in your meetings with the mother during this 3.75 hours, she told you many negative things about the father, correct?

Q: Some of them included the following?

- Junior did not have a good relationship with the father.
- Father is unstructured with all of the children.

(continued)

- *Father opposed to psychiatric treatment and psychotropic medication for Junior.*
- *Father has little to do with the two younger children.*
- *Father is rejecting of the daughter because he wanted a third son.*
- *Father does not have many friends.*
- *Other examples.*

Q: Doctor from this information, is it true that you form some initial impressions from the data that was presented to you?

Q: And is there some literature to the effect that psychiatrists frequently form diagnostic impressions very early in the clinical examination, sometimes in a matter of minutes?

Q: Is there a body of research showing that initial beliefs are often maintained, even in the face of counter evidence?

Q: Is there a body of literature indicating that once clinicians have taken a position or adopted a conclusion, that they apply very high standards of rigor in regard to any contradictory evidence and will accept a much lower standard of rigor from any data that supports their position?

Q: Doctor, are you familiar with the term "confirmatory bias"?

Q: Does that term refer to a tendency to form conclusions very early in the data collection process?

Q: Does it also refer to "a tendency of clinicians, and people in general, to maintain beliefs despite the force of counter evidence, and to pay particular attention to evidence that supports their beliefs, misinterpret ambiguous or nonsupportive evidence as supporting their beliefs, and disregard or dismiss counter evidence"?

Q: Doctor, are you familiar with the term "premature closure"?

Q: Does that term refer to a tendency to form conclusions very early in the data collection process?

Q: Does the literature show that this sometimes results in becoming resistant to data which might indicate that the initial conclusion was wrong?

Q: Doctor, you are familiar with the principal of primacy, correct?

Q: Does that refer to the tendency of people, when faced with conflicting stories, to believe that which they hear first?

Q: And we've established that you heard the mother for three and three-quarters of an hour during the initial interviews in your forensic analysis?

Q: Doctor, you are not claiming that because you are a psychiatrist, that like other humans, you are immune from the effects of confirmatory bias, premature closure, or the principle of primacy?

Q: In fact, doctor, on page 7 of your report, in this section entitled "Mental Status Exam," you present conclusions, findings, and impressions about the mother, correct?

Q: This was based upon just three and three-quarters of an hour of interviews with her, and when she brought the children to see you, all before you ever met or spoke to the father?

Q: In fact, doctor, you first saw the mother for the two-hour session on [date], true? And then you saw her for a second time on [date], true?

Q: It wasn't until two months after you first met the mother, and had a two-hour session with her, that you first met and spoke with the father?

Q: Doctor, you care about the people involved in the cases in which you act as a forensic evaluator?

Q: And even after you see an individual, you reflect upon the clinical examination, review your notes, and think about impressions and possible conclusions?

Q: You did this in the two-month interval between your initial interview with the mother and your initial interview with the father, correct?

(continued)

> Q: Doctor, you were the one who arranged the appointments in the sequence of events in connection with the forensic evaluation?
>
> Q: You determined who would be interviewed, the sequence of the interviews, the length of the interviews, the place of the interviews, the collateral sources that would be contacted, and other aspects of the forensic assignment ordered by Justice Johnson?
>
> Q: You had the option, did you not, of seeing each parent on the same day for the same amount of time?
>
> Q: You could have seen the mother for an hour and the father for an hour on the same date, correct?
>
> Q: Had you done that, you would have had input from both parents as part of the formulation of your initial impressions in your initial data collection?
>
> Q: Had you done this, you agree you would have ameliorated if not eliminated the effects of confirmatory bias, the principle of relevancy, and premature closure?

Psychological Testing

Psychological testing is often employed in forensic child custody/access evaluations, and there are myriad ways to challenge it. The cross examiner can usually establish that the testing is not a prime indicator of custodial fitness. The following colloquy took place during an actual case:

> Q: Doctor, you performed psychological testing of both parents, correct?
>
> A: Yes, the MMPI-2 and the Millon Clinical Multiaxial Inventory-III.
>
> Q: The psychological testing suggested some maladaptive personality disorder features of the mother, did it not?
>
> A: Yes.
>
> Q: This was in terms of certain personality traits?
>
> A: Yes.

Q: Doctor, am I correct that a personality trait or attribute basically is a habitual pattern of behavior?

A: Yes.

Q: When the traits are inflexible, they can become maladaptive and cause significant functional impairment, and then they become disorders, true?

A: Yes.

Q: The mother, according to the psychological testing, did have features of the excessive compulsive, histrionic, and sadistic personality attributes or traits, correct?

A: Correct.

Q: The excessive compulsive personality traits can manifest themselves in a variety of ways, correct?

A: Yes.

Q: Some features might be excessive orderliness, frugality and a cold mechanical quality and relationships with people, and being capable of a great amount of work or lacking flexibility and interpersonal warmth?

A: Yes, that can be part of it.

Q: A person with histrionic traits can often be self-centered, immature, vain, and at times exhibit dramatic behavior?

A: Yes.

Q: A sadistic personality trait can manifest itself by a lack of concern for people and deriving pleasure from harming or humiliating others?

A: That would be the definition of a sadist, but that is not what the test found. It just suggested there might be such traits related to sadism.

Q: In connection with the father, doctor, he was cooperative with the examinations?

A: Yes.

Q: The father received no clinical diagnosis, is that correct?

A: Yes.

(continued)

Q: *In fact, his clinical scales and content scores were within normal limits?*

A: *Yes.*

Q: *These conclusions were reached because psychological personality testing was done under the supervision of a clinical psychologist, true?*

A: *Yes.*

Q: *Not yourself?*

A: *No.*

Q: *Isn't it a fact that you were not present when the tests were administered?*

A: *That is correct.*

Q: *Doctor, it is true that the tests that were administered, the MMPI-2 and the Millon Clinical Multiaxial Inventory-III were not designed for, and have not been validated for, conventional custody issues?*

A: *That is true.*

Q: *In fact, your report indicates that the two tests administered are not designed to determine whether one parent is more suitable than the other?*

A: *Correct.*

Q: *And yet, the psychological test results must have some relevance or you would not have had them administered, true?*

A: *Yes.*

Q: *Doctor, do you recall that previously I questioned you about the practice parameters promulgated by the American Academy of Child and Adolescent Psychiatry?*

A: *I do recall.*

Q: *Those parameters state, and I quote, "In most cases, psychological testing of the parents is not required. Psychological tests, such as the Minnesota Multiphasic Personality Inventory, the Thematic Apperception Test, and the Rorschach were not designed for use in parenting evaluations. Their introduction into a legal process leads* the professionals battling over the meaning of raw data and attorneys making the most of findings of 'psychopathology,' but has little utility for assessing parenting." Doctor, you had one of those tests administered to the parents, correct?

A: Yes.

Q: That was the MMPI?

A: Yes.

Q: In fact, the same parameters also state, and again I quote, "Certain tests have been advanced as having specific utility in assessing variables specific to a custody evaluation. These include the Bricklin Perception of Relationships Test and the Ackerman–Schoendorf Scales for Parent Evaluation of Custody." You did not have either of these tests administered, isn't that a fact?

A: Yes.

Conclusion

Q: Doctor, there is a segment of your report entitled "Summary and Conclusions," correct?

A: Yes, it is near the end of my report.

Q: That section contains, does it not, your conclusions and opinions about the issues involved?

A: In part it does.

Q: Doctor, there is a difference between expert opinions and personal opinions, correct?

A: Yes.

Q: You understand, doctor, that in terms of professional opinions, it is implicit that the opinion be stated in terms of a reasonable degree of professional certainty?

A: That is my understanding of the standard.

Q: To give an opinion based upon reasonable degree of professional certainty, it must be grounded upon studies,

(continued)

research, literature in the field, and empirical data known to the mental health professional?

A: Yes.

Q: So what is known or relied upon by a mental health professional is that which is established empirically as reported in peer-reviewed professional literature, not what you as an individual may conclude idiosyncratically from intuition, or on the basis of personal value judgments?

A: Yes.

Q: In your extensive 40-page report, did you cite to the court any studies, literature, research, or empirical data?

A: No.

Q: Doctor, would you agree with me that different theoretical backgrounds of psychiatrists predispose them to reach different conclusions based upon the same data?

A: That can occur.

Business Valuation—Use of IRS Regulations

In cross examining a business valuation expert, it is essential that the cross examiner be familiar with and consider the relevant regulations promulgated by the Internal Revenue Service with respect to the valuation of closely held entities. These regulations act as guidelines for the appraiser and can provide a treasure trove of ammunition for cross examination. While there are numerous regulations affecting business valuations, the two primary regulations that the cross examiner must be familiar with, and which are reproduced as Appendices B and C, are as follows:

- Revenue Ruling 59-60, which has been recognized as "[O]ne of the most widely accepted and comprehensive approaches to the valuation of closely-held corporations."[32]
- Revenue Ruling 68-609, dealing with the capitalization of excess earnings method of valuation and sometimes referred to as the formula approach.

While this publication is not meant to present a detailed analysis of the revenue rulings, the salient consideration for the cross examiner is that he

---

32. *See, e.g.*, Kaye v. Kaye, 102 A.D.2d 682, 478 N.Y.S.2d 324 (2d Dept. 1984).

or she must check these regulations when reviewing the opposing expert's business valuation report. The cross examiner must explore whether the expert has departed from or violated the guidelines as set forth in the applicable revenue rulings. A few brief examples:

Q: Sir, you mentioned Revenue Ruling 59-60, is that correct?

A: Yes.

Q: That revenue ruling sets guidelines on the valuation of closely held businesses, correct?

A: Yes.

Q: Originally drafted to apply to estate and gift tax cases, but it has been applied to matrimonial cases as well?

A: Yes, it has.

Q: The revenue ruling sets forth eight factors that an appraiser should consider in valuing a closely held business?

A: Yes.

Q: And one of those factors is the earning capacity of the company?

A: Yes.

Q: Often the most important factor in valuing a closely held entity, true?

A: That's correct.

Q: Do you, as an appraiser, follow the guidelines promulgated in Revenue Ruling 59-60?

A: Yes.

Q: Did you do so in this case?

A: Yes.

Q: Certain of that?

A: Quite.

Q: Now, let me read to you, verbatim, from Revenue Ruling 59-60 from the commentary under the factor labeled the earning capacity of the company: "Detailed profit-and-loss

---

(continued)

statements should be obtained and considered for a representative period immediately prior to the required date of appraisal, preferably five or more years." In doing your appraisal, and calculating the value of Mr. C's business, you utilized a six-month interim statement of earnings for the year 2009, correct?

A: No. As I stated before, I considered the five years prior.

Q: Now let me repeat the question I posed to you very carefully with a request that you respond directly to my question. (Slowly) In doing your appraisal, and calculating the value of Mr. C's business, you utilized a six-month interim statement of earnings for the year 2009, correct?

A: Yes.

Q: How long has this corporation been in business?

A: Over 20 years.

Q: And Mr. C has been the sole shareholder of this corporation during that entire time?

A: Yes.

Q: And for each of the 20 years plus, tax returns and financial statements have been prepared which reflect the earnings of the company?

A: Yes.

Revenue Ruling 68-609, the capitalization of excess earnings method, is often utilized by appraisers in valuing closely held businesses and professional practices. Part of a cross examination of an appraiser utilizing this method may go as follows:

Q: You employed the capitalization of excess earnings approach to valuing my client's practice, is that correct?

A: Yes.

Q: As an experienced appraiser, you are aware that there are many different methods of valuing a business or professional practice?

A: Yes.

Q: There are valuation methods based upon the book value of a given business?

A: Yes.

Q: There are valuation methods based on the cost approach of a business?

A: Yes.

Q: There are valuation methods that are predicated upon a restrictive agreement such as a buy-sell and shareholder's agreement?

A: Yes.

Q: There are a number of valuation methods based upon the earnings of a particular business?

A: Yes.

Q: There is a discounted cash flow method of valuation?

A: Yes.

Q: There is a capitalization of earnings approach to valuation?

A: Yes.

Q: There is a capitalization of excess earnings approach to valuation?

A: Yes.

Q: And there are other methods of valuation that we have not mentioned, correct?

A: Yes.

Q: In fact, you used the capitalization of excess earnings approach in this case?

A: Yes.

Q: That is also known as the formula approach?

A: Yes.

Q: And it is set forth in Revenue Ruling 68-609, correct?

(continued)

A: That is correct.

Q: And you are familiar with Revenue Ruling 68-609?

A: Yes.

Q: You have read and reviewed it numerous times?

A: Yes.

Q: You have referred to this revenue ruling in numerous expert reports you have prepared, true?

A: Yes.

Q: Sir, I want to read to you, verbatim, from the closing sentence of Revenue Ruling 68-609: "Accordingly, the 'formula' approach may be used for determining the fair market value of intangible assets of a business only if there is no better basis therefor available." You are familiar with that language?

A: Yes.

Q: Of all the different approaches to valuation that you told us exist, you have used an approach that the applicable Revenue Ruling labels basically an approach of last resort?

A: I don't know if I would say that but the Revenue Ruling says what it says.

Many appraisers use an earnings-based approach to valuation, particularly where the subject entity sells or manufactures goods and services to the public. The cross examiner should explore the process that the appraiser uses to adjust the earnings (which they colloquially refer to as "normalizing the earnings" or "sanitizing the earnings") in detail. For example, suppose the appraiser has adjusted your client's earnings with respect to his automobile deductions, opining that 25 percent of the automobile expenses are personal in nature as opposed to appropriate business-related expenses. If there is a factual predicate for the appraiser to make that adjustment, then the adjustment would be valid. However, the adjustment cannot be made on supposition or speculation.

When the appraiser has averaged earnings over five years or some other period of years, you should inquire as to whether a weighted average would be appropriate, which would give greater weight to the more recent years because they are indicative of a trend in the earnings, either upward or downward. Straight averages are useful where the earnings are not greatly dissimilar from year to year. If you want a higher valuation and the appraiser has used a straight average of the earnings over a five-year continuum, where the two most recent years have shown significantly higher earnings, question the witness about a weighted average and have the witness do the math to show the higher average earnings that would result from using a weighted average of earnings.

An appraiser should not use abnormal, nonrecurring earnings or expenses as representative earnings for valuation purposes.[33] Consider the following cross examination:

> Q: You valued my client's personal injury law practice, correct?
>
> A: Yes.
>
> Q: One of the first steps in the valuation process is to average his earnings from the practice over a period of years?
>
> A: Yes.
>
> Q: You averaged my client's earnings from the law practice over a period of the last five years preceding the valuation date?
>
> A: Yes.
>
> Q: You used a straight average of the five years?
>
> A: Yes.
>
> Q: You did not eliminate or adjust any one of the five years before averaging the earnings over the five-year period?
>
> A: No, I did not.
>
> Q: The second year in the five-year spectrum, specifically 2007, my client's earnings were $912,000?
>
> A: Correct.
>
> Q: Comparing that to the other four years used in the average, the $912,000 was over $550,000 more than any other year, correct?
>
> A: Yes.

(continued)

---

33. Rev. Rul. 59-60, §4.02(d).

> Q: You are aware that this income was so large for that year because he settled the largest case of his career as a personal injury lawyer?
>
> A: Yes.
>
> Q: You made inquiry of his work in progress and his caseload over the years as part of your appraisal assignment?
>
> A: Yes.
>
> Q: You know that he does not have any other case in his past or current inventory of cases that approaches that case in terms of the amount expected to be recovered and the fee attached to such a case?
>
> A: That appears to be the case from my inquiry.
>
> Q: So the 2007 earnings would be abnormal, you agree?
>
> A: I would have to say they were.
>
> Q: You valued his practice utilizing Revenue Ruling 68-609, the formula approach, correct?
>
> A: Yes.
>
> Q: You are very familiar with that Revenue Ruling?
>
> A: Absolutely.
>
> Q: Let me quote from part of that Revenue Ruling: "The past earnings to which the formula is applied should fairly reflect the probable future earnings. Ordinarily, the period should not be less than five years, and abnormal years, whether above or below the average, should be eliminated." You did not adjust or eliminate the earnings from 2007 which you just told us was abnormal, correct?
>
> A: I would guess so.

Valuation Discounts

In a business valuation scenarios, once the appraiser has determined the value of the business based upon the applicable standard of valuation in the subject jurisdiction, generally either fair market value or fair value, the appraiser can apply a series of discounts. The discounts that the appraiser provides are often a fertile area for cross examination.

The most frequently applied discounts are:

- Discount for lack of marketability (DLOM), or illiquidity discount. This basically means that because shares of a closely held corporation cannot readily be sold, there is a discount for lack of marketability. Even a controlling interest in a closely held corporation may be unmarketable.[34]
- Minority discount. IRS Revenue Ruling 59-60(4)(g) provides that an appraiser must take into account "sales of the stock and the size of the block to be valued." This means that generally, a minority interest in a closely held entity lacks control and thus the value of the minority shareholding is discounted.
- Key person discount. A key person is "an individual whose contribution to a business is so significant that there is certainty that future earning levels will be adversely affected by the loss of the individual."[35] Accordingly, if there is no adequate plan for succession of management in the event of death or disability of such key person, a discount is applied.

When you are cross-examining an appraiser about the various discounts applicable to the subject case, she often will state that instead of applying a separate discount for, e.g., DLOM, she took into account lack of marketability in fixing the appropriate capitalization rate. Often, this answer becomes somewhat of a garbage pail when you ask the appraiser why she did or did not take into account certain factors and discounts. Don't let the appraiser get away with such an answer. An attack may be as follows:

Q: Mr. Appraiser, you are aware that my client owns a 20 percent share in ABC Corporation?

A: Yes.

Q: That is a minority interest, correct?

A: Yes.

Q: His fellow shareholder and the president and CEO of the company, Mr. Bigshot, owns 80 percent, correct?

A: Yes.

Q: As such, Mr. Bigshot has control of the company?

A: You can say that, but he relies upon your client very much.

(continued)

---

34. Est. of Gray v. Commissioner,73 T.C.M. 1940 (1997).
35. IRS Valuation Training for Appeals Officers Coursebook, 1998.

Q: Whether he does or not, he can effectively fire my client as an employee of the company, should he so desire?

A: Yes.

Q: He can decide to obtain additional financing debt for the company, or to merge the company with another company without my client consenting to these actions?

A: Technically, yes.

Q: In reality yes, correct?

A: I guess so.

Q: You are familiar with the concept of a minority discount?

A: Yes.

Q: In valuation methodology, a minority discount is applied where the shareholder lacks control, correct?

A: That is part of it, yes.

Q: In your report, I notice that there is no reference to a minority discount, true?

A: The report does not mention it specifically.

Q: Isn't it a fact that you failed to apply a minority discount, even though my client lacks control?

A: Actually, no. I took his minority status into account in formulating the applicable capitalization rate that I utilized in connection with the capitalization of excess earnings method.

Q: So, you made some quantitative finding about the minority discount that affected the capitalization rate?

A: Yes.

Q: Did this quantitative finding lower or raise the capitalization rate?

A: It raised the capitalization rate and thus lowered the multiplier applied to the excess earnings that I capitalized.

Q: By what amount did the inclusion of a factor for a minority discount raise the capitalization rate?

A: I can't say specifically.

Q: Can you tell us approximately?

A: Oh, I would assume about 10 percent.

Q: You assume, but the question I am asking is if you know?

A: I can't say with specificity.

Q: So, although you state that you took into account the minority discount, all you can tell us is an assumption as to the quantification of the discount, and you can't tell us the exact amount of the quantification that you assumed?

A: I believe I have answered your questions regarding the minority discount.

22

Expert Testimony: Reliability of Scientific Expert Testimony

The reliability of scientific evidence is overlooked as a fertile area for cross examination in the field of family law. However, you can test the reliability of any scientific evidence propounded by an expert under applicable federal and state standards.

Since *Frye v. United States*,[36] and as is still the rule in some jurisdictions, expert testimony based on scientific principles or procedures is admissible only after the relevant scientific community has generally accepted the underlying device, procedure, or methodology. Accordingly, cases often require so-called Frye hearings before or during trial to determine whether the expert's methodologies are accepted as reliable within the scientific community. General acceptance does not mean that the particular procedure is unanimously endorsed by scientists, but rather that it is generally accepted as reliable. Moreover, even though the expert is using reliable principles and methods and is extrapolating from reliable data, a court may exclude the expert's opinion under the Frye test if there is simply too great an analytical gap between the data and the opinion proffered.[37]

---

36. Frye v. United States, 293 F.2d 1013 (D.C. Cir. 1923).
37. Cornell v. 360 West 51st Street Realty, LLC, 22 N.Y.3d 762, 986 N.Y.S.2d 389 (2014).

After *Frye*, the federal courts adopted *Daubert v. Merrell Dow Pharmaceuticals, Inc.*[38] In rejecting the *Frye* standard, the court held that expert testimony must reflect scientific knowledge and it must assist the trier of fact. Thus, it is the function of the judge, as a gatekeeper, to assure that scientific evidence is reliable and proceeds from scientific knowledge.[39] The Daubert court developed four factors to help determine the reliability of a particular scientific theory or procedure—testing, peer review, error rates, and "acceptability" in the relevant scientific community—which might prove helpful in determining the reliability of a particular scientific theory or techniques.[40] The four-part test more specifically includes the following:

- *Is the theory or method subject to testing or falsifiability?* "A key question to be answered in determining whether a theory or technique is scientific knowledge that will assist the trier of fact will be whether it can be (and has been) tested. 'Scientific methodology today is based on generating hypotheses and testing them to see if they can be falsified; indeed, this methodology is what distinguishes science from other fields of human inquiry.'"[41]
- *Has the theory or technique been subjected to peer review and publication?* "Submission to the scrutiny of the scientific community is a component of 'good science,' in part because it increases the likelihood that substantive flaws in methodology will be detected."[42]
- *What is the rate of error?* "[I]n the case of a particular scientific technique, the court ordinarily should consider the known or potential rate of error."[43]
- *Is it generally accepted by the relevant scientific community?* "'General acceptance' can yet have a bearing on the inquiry. A 'reliability assessment does not require, although it does permit, explicit identification of a relevant scientific community and an express determination of a particular degree of acceptance within that community.'"[44]
- In *Kumho Tire Company, Ltd., v. Carmichael*,[45] the principles of Daubert were extended by the Court, which commented that:

---

38. 509 U.S. 579, 589, 113 S.Ct. 2786, 125 L.Ed.2d 469 (1993).

39. Fed. Rules of Evidence, § 702.

40. Kumho Tire Company, Ltd., v. Carmichael, 526 U.S. 137, 119 S.Ct. 1167 (1999).

41. KENNETH R. FOSTER, JUDGING SCIENCE: SCIENTIFIC KNOWLEDGE AND THE FEDERAL COURTS (Reprint Ed. 1999).

42. THOMAS BUCKLES, LAWS OF EVIDENCE (1st Ed. 2002).

43. Daubert v. Merrell Dow Pharms., Inc., 509 U.S. 579, 596, 113 S. Ct. 2786 (Sup. Ct., U.S. 1993).

44. *Id.*

45. 26 U.S. 137, 119 S.Ct. 1167 (1999).

> *We conclude that Daubert's general holding—setting forth*
> *the trial judge's general "gatekeeping" obligation—applies*
> *not only to testimony based on "scientific" knowledge,*
> *but also to testimony based on "technical" and "other*
> *specialized" knowledge.* See Fed. Rule Evid. 702. We
> also conclude that a trial court may consider one
> or more of the more specific factors that Daubert
> mentioned when doing so will help determine
> that testimony's reliability. But, as the Court stated
> in Daubert, the test of reliability is "flexible," and
> Daubert's list of specific factors neither necessarily
> nor exclusively applies to all experts or in every case.
> Rather, the law grants a district court the same broad
> latitude when it decides how to determine reliability
> as it enjoys in respect to its ultimate reliability
> determination. See General Electric Co. v. Joiner, 522
> U.S. 136, 143, 118 S.Ct. 512, 139 L.Ed.2d 508 (1997)
> (courts of appeals are to apply "abuse of discretion"
> standard when reviewing district court's reliability
> determination). (Emphasis added.)

You can often challenge an expert's use of scientific theory or procedures in child custody litigation where mental health professionals opined based upon psychological testing, various syndromes, theories of child development, and the like. Research all of the particular theory's testing, with emphasis on two aspects: reliability and validity. For example, a frequently used clinical test in child custody cases is the MMPI/MMPI-2, where a high score on a particular clinical scale is statistically associated with certain behavioral characteristics. This test is generally thought to produce high reliability. However, because it is a personality questionnaire, people may answer questions in a manner they deem socially desirable or acceptable, as opposed to being completely truthful. This can distort the reliability and validity of the test results.

Start preparing early in the case for this type of attack, because a challenge based upon either *Frye* or *Daubert* is often subject to a motion in limine, with a hearing held prior to the commencement of the trial in chief. Begin your challenge under *Frye* or *Daubert* when you receive the adverse expert's report and notice that your adversary is retaining a less than reputable expert.[46]

---

46. For an excellent analysis of how to confront expert testimony, see JOHN A. ZERVO-POULOS, CONFRONTING THE MENTAL HEALTH EVIDENCE: A PRACTICAL GUIDE TO RELIABIL-ITY AND EXPERTS IN FAMILY LAW (2009).

Bibliography

ABA Section on Litigation, The Art of Cross Examination: Essays from the Bench and Bar (ABA Publishing, 2014).

John Nicholas Iannuzzi, Handbook of Cross Examination: The Mosaic Art (Prentice Hall, 1999).

Larry S. Pozner and Roger J. Dodd, Cross Examination: Science and Techniques, 2d Ed. (Lexis Nexis, 2004).

Francis L. Wellman, The Art of Cross Examination (The MacMillan Company, 1905).

Appendix A
Cross-Examination of a Forensic Psychiatrist

Noncompliance with Order of Referral

Q: Doctor, your involvement in this case emanated from a court order by Justice Ashton?

A: Correct.

Q: And that order appointed you and set forth your assignment and obligations in connection with the forensic evaluation, correct?

A: Yes.

Q: That order by Justice Ashton set forth findings that you were required to make and findings which you were directed not to make, correct?

A: Yes.

Q: And in performing this forensic evaluation, you considered all the relevant facts?

A: I believe I did.

Q: To the extent you did not do so, your evaluation would not be complete, true?

A: Yes.

Q: Your methodology was complete?

A: I believe it was.

Q: To the extent it was not complete, it would be wrong and less reliable?

A: Yes.

Q: Your investigation in methodology was fair?

A: I believe it was.

Q: To the extent it was not fair, it would be inappropriate?

A: Yes.

Q: Doctor, you note on page 2 of your report, under the heading "Reason for Referral," the directions to Justice Ashton as to the topics and scope of your assignment in this case?

A: Correct.

Q: When you undertook this assignment, did you consider yourself bound by the order of Justice Ashton as to what you were to do?

A: Yes.

Q: Did you carry out that order in both the letter and spirit?

A: Yes.

Q: For example, you are directed not to make a specific recommendation as to legal custody?

A: That is part of the order, correct.

Q: Justice Ashton directed you to address "suggested parent access times including overnight visits"?

A: Yes.

Q: Doctor, isn't it a fact that your 32-page, single-spaced report contains no "suggested parent access times including overnight visits" as directed by Justice Ashton?

A: In specific terms, no.

Q: You did not do that in any terms, isn't that correct, doctor?

A: I guess you are right.

Q: The order of Justice Ashton also directed you to address "suggested decision-making roles of each parent," correct?

A: Yes.

Q: Again, doctor, a perusal of your report fails to contain any suggested decision-making roles of each parent, true?

A: Let me see. It appears that way.

Q: The order of Justice Ashton also directs that you address "suggested spheres of influence"?

A: Yes.

Q: And your report fails to address that direction by Justice Ashton as well?

A: I guess so.

Q: Doctor, as a forensic evaluator appointed by a court pursuant to a court order, do you believe you have the right to ignore any of the directions made by the court in its order of referral question?

A: No.

Q: And yet, doctor, we have just noted three areas that you were directed to address and which you failed to do so?

A: It appears that way.

Experience in Testifying

For more information, see Chapter 21, page 93.

Qualifications, Board Certification, and Experience

Q: Doctor, at the commencement of your direct examination, you told the court of your qualifications and the court received into evidence your curriculum vitae, correct?

A: Yes.

Q: *I note that you told the court that you are board certified in adult, child, and forensic psychiatry?*

A: *Correct.*

Q: *Research has not demonstrated a relationship between board certification and competence, has it?*

A: *Not to my knowledge.*

Q: *Has it been demonstrated through published scientific research that the conclusions of board-certified psychiatrists are more accurate than those of psychiatrists who lack board certification?*

A: *I am not aware of any such research.*

Q: *Are there a number of publications and reputable psychiatric journals to the effect that no relationship between board certification and competence has been established?*

A: *I am not aware of that either.*

Q: *Isn't board certification defined by the board as indicating only minimal competence in the field?*

A: *Well, you have to pass a test, so I don't think it is "minimal."*

Q: *And doctor, you are certified in forensic psychiatry as well?*

A: *Yes.*

Q: *This is a relatively new kind of certification, is it not?*

A: *Yes.*

Q: *Similarly, it has not been demonstrated through research that such certification indicates that a person has a higher level of competence or more accurate conclusions than those not so certified, has it?*

A: *I am not aware of any such research.*

Professional Association Protocols

Q: *Doctor, you have been practicing psychiatry for many years now?*

A: *Yes.*

Q: During that period of time, you have been a member of the American Academy of Child and Adolescent Psychiatry, correct?

A: I am a member, yes.

Q: In fact, you have been an active member, serving on various committees of that association?

A: Correct.

Q: You are familiar with the fact that the American Academy of Child and Adolescent Psychiatry promulgates guidelines for its members who are engaged in forensic psychiatry?

A: Yes.

Q: Specifically, the professional organization published a Summary of Practice Parameters for Child Evaluation?

A: Yes.

Q: As a long-time active member of this association, you are familiar with these guidelines?

A: In a general sense, yes.

Q: You have employed these guidelines in your practice?

A: I believe I have.

Q: You have employed these guidelines in connection with the forensic evaluation in this case?

A: Again, I believe I have.

Q: Doctor, in those parameters, it states, and I quote: "The evaluator should consider meeting with the parents together at least once if the parties consent to it." It is a fact that you never met with the parents together and you did not seek consent to a joint meeting with the parents?

A: That is correct.

Q: It further states: "Explore any allegations parents make against each other," correct?

A: Yes.

Q: Doctor, is it a fact that my client made a number of allegations against his wife, particularly with respect to her alcoholism, that you did not explore?

A: I believe I took up these allegations with the mother.

Q: If you did, that would be included in what you have described as a comprehensive report that you rendered to the court, correct?

A: Yes.

Q: Can you point to that part of the report, doctor, which describes your exploration of my client's allegations and specifically a discussion of same with the mother?

A: I believe inferentially it is discussed in my general discussion about the mother's alcoholism.

Q: Doctor, in those same practice parameters, in the section entitled "Structuring the Evaluation," it tells the examiner to request all legal documents from both sides, reading them not for the truth of the contents but, rather, for insight into what the parties are charging and counter-charging, correct?

A: You seem to have them in front of you, so I am sure it is correct.

Q: Doctor, in the section of your report entitled "Review of Records," which goes from pages 26 through 29, you list eight records that you reviewed, correct?

A: Yes.

Q: And you agree with me, doctor, that none of them include the legal documents from either or both sides of this controversy?

A: Yes.

Q: Doctor, those same practice parameters state that the examiner should "consider interviewing extended family, friends, neighbors, and alternate caregivers, such as babysitters," correct?

A: Again, I am sure it so states.

Q: You did not interview any extended family, friends, or neighbors of either of the parents, true?

A: True.

Q: Doctor, although your report states on page 3 that the family had live-in help until one year ago, and there is a full-time sitter Monday through Friday with variable hours, you did not interview any such person, correct?

A: Correct.

Q: Those same parameters state "Consider whether a visit to one or both homes would be helpful." Did you visit the home of the parties?

A: No, I did not believe that was necessary.

Failure to Contact School Psychologist for Child

Q: Doctor, in doing your forensic analysis, is it important that you do as complete an analysis as possible?

Q: You want to gather as much pertinent information about the subject of your report as is possible, correct?

Q: Did you strive to do that the present case?

Q: Doctor, there is an important difference between an expert opinion and a personal opinion?

Q: The defining attribute of an expert opinion is that the procedures employed in formulating the opinion use the body of knowledge that forms the foundation upon which those procedures were developed, correct?

Q: You agree, do you not, that if the accumulated knowledge in your field was not utilized, the opinion expressed would not be an expert opinion, but rather a personal opinion, albeit one being expressed by an expert?

Q: Forensic experts are expected to investigate the accuracy of information provided by those being evaluated, correct?

Q: You are court-appointed correct, doctor?

Q: Would you agree as a general proposition that the fact that an expert is court-appointed does not guarantee either objectivity or impartiality?

Q: In attempting to do a complete analysis, would mental health professionals who had interaction with Peter Jr. be important persons to contact?

Q: Such a person will be deemed a collateral contact?

Q: If you did contact such person it would be noted in your report, correct?

Q: Doctor, in your report you note that Peter Jr. is in a socialization program and sees school psychologist Julia Cohen weekly?

A: Yes.

Q: You agree with me, doctor, that the school psychologist thereby has very frequent contact with Peter Jr.?

A: I assume so, at least weekly, as it states.

Q: And this frequent contact is in the school setting, correct?

A: Yes.

Q: And the school psychologist would presumably have access to information concerning the child's school performance, interaction with his peers, input from the child's teachers, classroom behavior, test scores and grades for the child, and other pertinent information that could bear upon your assessment in this case?

Q: Doctor, do you see in your report, and I'm referencing page 19 and consecutive pages, you note the collateral contacts that you contacted and spoke with in connection with this case?

A: Yes.

Q: You note that you had a telephone conference with a psychologist who treated Peter Jr. three years ago?

Q: You are aware that the school psychologist, Julia Cohen, sees Peter Jr. weekly and on an ongoing basis, including at the present time?

Q: You also note that another collateral contact was a substance abuse counselor of the mother?

Q: You also note that you spoke with a Doctor Burke, who treated Peter Jr. and other family members?

Q: This was done in private sessions outside of the school setting, correct?

Q: Doctor, you did not have any direct contact, by telephone or otherwise, with the school psychologist of Peter Jr., namely, Julia Cohen?

Q: Will you agree with me that the thoughts and observations of a school psychologist who saw the child weekly and had access to the child's school records and performance, and interaction with his peers, would be pertinent to a full and complete assessment of this child for the purposes of your forensic evaluation?

Q: In fact, you did not even attempt to contact the school psychologist, did you?

Q: So, at least in that respect, your report is not as complete as it should have been or what you would have liked it to have been?

Q: And this court will not have the benefit of this pertinent information in making its assessment as to the custody of Peter Jr.?

Q: In your initial interview with the mother, on page 3 of your report, did she tell you that there is tremendous tension in the house because "there is little or no agreement between the parents about how to parent Peter Jr."?

Q: So the issue of parenting of Peter Jr. was a major stressor to this entire family, correct?

Q: So collecting and analyzing all of the pertinent information about Peter Jr. would be all the more important, correct?

Law Guardian (Attorney for Child)

Q: Doctor, the report you issued in this case, was it a comprehensive report?

A: I believe so.

Q: You included all of the facts that you considered relevant in your evaluation?

A: Yes.

Q: You reviewed the report before you submitted it to the court?

A: Yes.

Q: And you reviewed it again before you testified in court today?

A: I reviewed it yesterday.

Q: Do you still believe it is comprehensive and states all the relevant facts?

A: Yes.

Q: You are aware that the court appointed an attorney for the children, Mr. Prince?

A: Yes.

Q: In that capacity, you know that he regularly communicated with the children and acted as the children's advocate?

A: Yes.

Q: Mr. Prince then might have had important information to impart that would be relevant to your comprehensive evaluation?

A: Yes, he certainly might.

Q: There is no reference in your report, doctor, to you having met with or conversed with Mr. Prince?

A: I guess there is not.

Q: So whatever relevant information he may have had, you were not privy to it?

A: No.

Q: And it was not contained in what you have described as a comprehensive report?

A: No.

Peer Review

For more information, see Chapter 17, page 75.

Confirmatory Bias and the Principle of Primacy

For more information, see Chapter 21, page 125.

Alcoholism

For more information, see Chapter 21, page 145.

Joint Custody

Q: Doctor, you have stated, have you not, and specifically on page 31 of your report, that each parent is capable of providing suitable residential care for the children?

A: Yes.

Q: Would you also agree that both parents are loving and caring of their children?

A: Yes.

Q: And doctor, would you agree with me that where you have two loving and caring parents, each capable of providing suitable residential care, it is best if both parents are intimately and extensively involved in the upbringing and entire maturation process of the children?

A: Unquestionably.

[* Indicates that you should ask this question only if joint custody is a feasible choice.]

Q: Doctor, as stated of page 31 of your report, and I quote: "both parties are capable of providing suitable residential care." Those are your words, correct?*

A: Yes.

Q: Doctor, I am making reference to page 3 of your report where on you quote the mother stating as follows: "on weekends, we take care of the kids without the sitter." Doctor, will you concede that when the mother said that, the reference to "we" meant herself and the father of the children?*

A: Yes, I so quoted her.

Q: You reported to this court on page 14 of your report that Jr. "has a good relationship with both parents," correct?*

A: Correct.

Q: You noted on page 15 of your report, and you highlighted it, that Jr. expressed no preference?*

A: Yes.

Q: You further noted that the son, Alan, believes it would be fair to split time with each parent, and quoted him as saying, "I am pretty organized so it would be no problem"?*

A: Yes.

Q: You also noted on page 17 that Alan was emphatic that the future arrangements would not be confusing to him and he could handle a physical custody split, which he thought to be the fairest?*

A: I so noted.

Q: You noted, did you not, that there is strong agreement between the parents that Alan is a competitive, athletic, and assertive boy who is generally well-adjusted?*

A: Yes.

Q: You also noted that there is a strong consensus between the parents about Beth's anxiety problems, psychological and interpersonal strengths, and her array of age-appropriate interests?*

A: Yes.

Q: You noted at the top of page 25 that "it is significant that there is a high degree of consensus between the parents concerning the nature of Peter's psychiatric problems, his social, emotional, and behavioral symptoms, and his strengths and weaknesses in terms of school, interests, and socialization." Is this correct?

A: I did.

Q: So you found that the parents agree as to these issues?

A: Yes, I did.

Q: Doctor, there are not many perfect parents, are there?

A: No.

Q: Many parents have some characteristics that are less than desirable, is this not correct?

A: Certainly.

Q: In most cases, children manage to accomplish reasonably normal development anyway, is that not correct?

A: That is correct.

Q: Aside from Peter Jr., who we know suffers from Asperger's syndrome and PPD, the other children did not show any signs of any serious psychological problems, correct?

A: No, they did not.

Q: And these children have been living with both parents all of their lives, true?

A: True.

Q: In fact, they are doing pretty well, considering the marital discord in the home, would you agree?

A: Yes.

Q: Would that suggest to you that the children are psychologically sound?

A: In a sense, but there are the problems that I have noted.

Q: And they would likely do all right with either of the parents, or with both of the parents in a joint custody arrangement, is that correct?

A: I do not believe that joint custody is feasible in this case. In a sense, I wish it was. However, there is a long history of the inability of these two parents to act in concert and harmony, even for the benefit of their children.

Q: Would joint custody be more fitting for adolescents who arrive at a point in life where parents are less likely to have influence on their development, and peer associations are considerably more influential?

A: Possibly.

Stressors and the Examiner Effect

Q: Doctor, you had multiple examinations of the parents and the children, correct? [Recount the visits and clinical examinations.]

Q: And when you did this, doctor, did you have any doubt in your mind that the children knew the purpose for which they were coming to your office?

Q: They knew that their parents were embroiled in a divorce action, which included the issue of which parent they would live with when the action was completed?

Q: Would you state that both the parents and the children, when they met with you, were under a certain amount of stress and anxiety because of the circumstances surrounding their visits with you?

Q: Doctor, is there a very substantial body of scientific and professional literature indicating that the general circumstances under which a forensic examination is conducted (the time, the place, the purpose) affects the kind of information or data that emerges in the examination?

Q: Doctor, isn't there research showing that such factors affect the kind of information that is obtained in the interview?

Q: Isn't there described in the literature something known as situation effects?

Q: The pendency of a divorce and custody case could qualify as such a situational effect, correct?

Q: In fact, the DSM describes marital breakup as a psychosocial problem that can affect diagnosis and prognosis?

Q: The breakup of a marriage, particularly when children are involved, is a highly stressful situation for most normal people, both parents and children, right?

Q: The behavior observed under the circumstances may not be representative of the individual's behavior under more normal, less highly stressful circumstances, true?

Q: Not only do we have the strain of the circumstances relating to the divorce and the issue of custody, but the additional strain of the circumstance of the clinical examination itself?

Q: Doctor, in addition to the psychological stress of a divorce and custody proceeding, is it not a fact that a clinical examination is also affected by the nature of the examiner himself or herself?

Q: The attitudes of the examiner, the personality of the examiner, the race or economic status of the subject and the examiner, all have an effect, correct?

Q: You have learned in your studies, doctor, have you not, that some examiners with one theoretical orientation might get different data, record different data, and interpret the data differently than an examiner of a different theoretical orientation, correct?

Q: Similarly, examiners with different personalities might get some different kinds of information from the people they examine, true?

Q: This is because people respond differently to different types of people, true?

Q: What the examiner perceives, remembers, and records is also subject to various influences?

Q: There may be distortion or bias due to the theoretical orientation of the examiner, the values and attitudes of the examiner, and other characteristics of the examiner?

Q: The interpretation of the data collected is subject to influence, distortion, and bias due to the same factors, am I correct?

Q: In addition, forensic evaluation cases like this necessarily involve a prediction?

Q: And doctor, isn't it a fact that a prediction in this field is overwhelmingly speculative?

Q: And one examiner or clinician can base his or her conclusions on unvalidated and speculative theories of child development that differ from another examiner or clinician?

Q: There are different and competing theories of child development?

Q: And doctor, what you have provided us with on your direct examination is what could be called a clinical judgment, is that not correct?

Q: And isn't there a substantial body of scientific and professional literature indicating that there are a number of serious flaws and problems with clinical judgment (i.e., that it lacks validity or cannot be relied upon)?

Facts Favorable to the Father

Q: As noted on page 10 of your report, the father was subjected to four child protective investigations?

A: Yes.

Q: All of the investigations concluded with an "unfounded" finding, correct?

A: Yes.

Q: He believes the referrals were one from the school and the rest from his wife or her mother, and he so told you?

A: Yes.

Q: Did you explore this allegation with the mother?

A: Not really.

Q: Would it be pertinent if she made false allegations of child abuse or neglect?

A: Of course.

Q: So in not exploring this allegation, your report is incomplete in another respect, correct?

A: Yes.

Q: With respect to the father, there is no family history of psychiatric illness, alcoholism, or substance abuse?

A: That is correct.

Q: You noted that the father "presents as pleasant, articulate, and cooperative"?

A: I did.

Q: Peter Jr. again mentions how much he enjoys building rockets which he shoots at a site in upstate New York?

A: Yes, he does

Q: With whom does he do this?

A: His father.

Q: You note in your report on page 18 that Jr. seemed "closely identified to his dad as they share a love of trains and rockets" and that Mr. Smith tries to reassure Jr. when he gets fixated on a particular issue which causes him to become anxious or angry?

A: I did.

Q: You also noted that Mr. Smith tried to diffuse the issue about summer camp in noting that he, too, must abide by the court ruling?

A: Yes, that was very appropriate.

Q: When Jr. argued that he should be able to fire his doctor, his father gently, but firmly, said that does not work that way, to which Alan concurred, correct?

A: Yes.

Q: That also was an appropriate and proper way to handle the situation?

A: I believe so.

Q: You also noted on page 19 that "Mr. Smith stayed clear of any hot button issues involving himself and Carol, which showed good judgment on his part in front of the children"?

A: Yes, I so noted.

Q: As part of your psychological testing, you performed the MMPI-2 tests on the parents, correct?

A: Yes.

Q: And the results regarding the father showed no clinical diagnoses, true?

A: Yes.

Q: His clinical scales and content scores were within normal limits?

A: Yes, that is what the test revealed.

Q: With respect to Mr. Smith the test revealed features of obsessive-compulsive, histrionic, and sadistic personality attributes?

A: Yes.

Q: Doctor, if you would be good enough to turn to page 23 of your report, I notice that you put certain words in bold print; is that for emphasis to the reader?

A: Yes.

Q: Now, you bold type the words "open and cooperative manner" when you speak of Dr. Smith's approach to the testing, correct?

A: Yes.

Q: Two paragraphs later, you state that "Mr. Smith was cooperative with the examination," correct?

A: Yes.

Q: You chose not to put his cooperation with the tests in bold type, it is in regular type?

A: Yes.

Q: So you chose to emphasize the mother's cooperation but not the father's?

A: It appears so.

Q: On the same page, you put in bold type, and referring to the mother, the words "disciplined in nature, often appearing to be conscientious, dependable, and persistent," correct?

A: Yes.

Q: Those are basically positive traits of the mother that you are emphasizing?

A: Correct.

Q: With respect to the sentence: "Dr. Smith did have features of obsessive-compulsive, histrionic, and sadistic personality traits," you chose not to emphasize that sentence and therefore it was not in bold type?

A: Yes.

Q: That sentence portrays a basically negative statement about Dr. Smith, does it not?

A: It depends upon the degree of each of these traits, but generally speaking, they are not positive, albeit many very successful people have, for example, obsessive-compulsive personality traits.

Q: At the bottom of page 23 and carrying over to page 24, you put in bold type, and referring to the father, "Interpersonal relationships may be shallow in nature and there may be a tendency for such an individual to appear self-centered and exploitive or indifferent to the needs of others"?

A: I did place that in bold type.

Q: Again, for emphasis?

A: Yes.

Q: So, doctor, you deliberately chose to put the father's negative findings in bold type for emphasis and the mother's positive findings in bold type for emphasis?

A: It appears that way.

Q: This is in spite of the fact that the findings from the psychological testing included positive and negative features about both parents, correct?

A: Yes.

Availability

Q: Doctor, a parent's availability to be with the children as frequently as possible is a factor to be considered in a custody determination, do you agree?

A: Yes, it is one factor to consider.

Q: In this case, we have two working parents, both working full time, correct?

A: Yes.

Q: You noted in your report on page 2 that occasionally the mother worked 24-hour shifts at the hospital, correct?

A: Yes.

Q: You are aware doctor, are you not, that my client works a normal work week, namely, Monday through Friday?

A: Yes.

Q: You further noted that until a year ago, they had full-time help in the house and since that time a full-time sitter, Monday through Friday?

A: Correct.

Q: In your report you cited the mother's statement that on weekends, "we" take care of the kids without the sitter?

A: Yes.

Q: So you would agree, would you not, that at least as work schedules are concerned, the father is available at least as much as the mother if not more so?

A: Yes.

Psychological Tests

For more information, see Chapter 21, page 128.

Collateral Sources

Q: Doctor, would it be fair to say that you rely to a great extent upon the collateral contacts in this case?

A: I relied to some extent, I would not say great extent.

Q: You expend about four pages in your report discussing the collateral sources, true?

A: Yes.

Q: They included a clinical psychologist who treated Peter Jr. about three years ago, Doctor Lois Lane, mentioned on page 20?

A: Yes.

Q: Your only contact with her was a phone consultation on August 6, 2008, correct?

A: That is correct.

Q: You had no in-person meeting with her?

A: No.

Q: How long did that telephone call last?

A: I don't recall specifically, but maybe about 15 minutes or so.

Q: Did you take notes?

Q: Do you have in court with you today the original notes? (If not, explore.)

Q: Would it be fair to say that after that phone conversation, it was clear to you that she liked the mother and disliked the father?

A: I don't know if she personalized it that way. She did have her views of the parents, however.

Q: Am I correct in saying you received no documents from her?

A: That is correct.

Q: You did not read or review any notes she took or may have taken during her sessions with Peter Jr., or the parents, or any recordings she may have made?

A: No.

Q: So basically, you took her word for what she said without any form of cor-roboration through original notes or other data?

A: I had no reason to doubt what she told me, which were her professional opinions and judgments.

Q: Did you ever know or converse with this clinician prior to that phone call?

A: No.

Q: Were you familiar with her reputation within the professional mental health community?

A: No.

Q: So whether she was an accomplished and highly respected mental health professional, or a quack, you had no way of knowing?

A: I believe I would have discerned if she was, to use your word, a "quack."

Q: You also had a phone consultation with Doctor Trisha Burke on August 8, 2008?

A: Yes.

Q: How long did that conversation last?

A: Again, I am not sure, but probably about the same length as the phone call we just discussed.

Q: Did you ever meet in person with Doctor Burke about this case?

A: No.

Q: Did you receive any notes or documentation from Doctor Burke concerning her treatment of Peter Jr.?

A: No.

Q: Again, did you take her word for what she said without any form of cor-roboration or validation?

A: I considered what she said along with all the other information that was imparted to me as part of this forensic assignment.

Q: You are aware that Doctor Burke and the father had differences of opinion as to the proper treatment for Peter Jr., including drugs that were administered for his use?

A: Yes, I was made aware of that.

Q: These differences of opinion might have led to a bias on the part of Doctor Burke against the father and in favor of the mother?

A: I assume that is possible.

Q: But you would not know if such a bias existed or not, correct?

A: True.

Q: You don't advocate, do you, that every parent should blindly follow whatever advice a therapist gives if, in apparent good faith, there is reason to believe that the advice may be against the interest of the child?

A: No. Blind adherence is certainly not optimum.

Q: Am I correct in concluding that based upon the conversation with Doctor Burke, there is a general dislike between her and the father?

A: I would not know if it was on such a personal level, although they did have disagreements about treatment and drugs which were prescribed for Peter Jr.

Q: In the "Recommendation to the Court" section of your report, you state doctor, that "the observations of Drs. L and G, who have worked with the family for several years, seem highly relevant to reaching a conclusion about custody, especially decision-making authority"?

A: I said that.

Q: It is clear then, doctor, that you relied heavily upon the observations of Doctors L and G in formulating your own conclusions?

A: It appears that way, yes.

Q: Doctor, while recognizing that you are not a lawyer, although you have had extensive courtroom experience, you are aware of what is known as hearsay evidence, true?

A: I have heard the term many times.

Q: *Hearsay, to your understanding, is basically out-of-court statements to prove a relevant fact in the case, correct?*

A: *I believe that is what it is.*

Q: *And you agree with me that the portion of your report relating to the observations and statements of Doctor L and Doctor G are out-of-court statements which render opinions upon which you have relied?*

A: *To the extent I have previously said, yes.*

Q: *Doctor, we have you relying extensively on the substance of telephone conversations which first, are hearsay and, second, have not been corroborated or validated by you by even the acquisition of notes or other original data?*

A: *Yes.*

Q: *Do you believe that such extensive reliance on this type of material is conducive to the rendering of a comprehensive, accurate report to be submitted to a court to aid in the determination of a child custody dispute?*

A: *I believe on balance I have rendered such a report.*

Conclusions

Q: *Doctor, there is a segment of your report entitled "Summary and Conclusions," correct?*

A: *Yes, it is near the end of my report.*

Q: *And that section contains, does it not, your conclusions and opinions about the issues involved?*

A: *In part it does.*

Q: *Doctor, there is a difference between expert opinions and personal opinions, correct?*

A: *Yes.*

Q: *You understand, doctor, that in terms of professional opinions, it is implicit that the opinion be stated in terms of reasonable professional certainty?*

A: *That is my understanding of the standard.*

Q: And to give an opinion based upon reasonable professional certainty, it must be grounded upon studies, research, literature in the field, and empirical data known to the mental health professional?

A: Yes.

Q: So what is known or relied upon by a mental health professional is that which is established empirically as reported in peer-reviewed professional literature, not what you as an individual may conclude idiosyncratically from intuition, or on the basis of personal value judgments?

A: Yes.

Q: In your extensive 32-page report, did you cite to the court any studies, literature, research, or empirical data?

A: No.

Q: Doctor, would you agree with me that psychiatrists' different theoretical backgrounds predispose them to reach different conclusions based upon the same data?

A: That can occur.

Attorney: Thank you, doctor, I have no further questions.

Appendix B
Revenue Ruling 59-60

Rev. Rul. 59-60, 1959-1 CB 237—IRC Sec. 2031 (Also Section 2512.)
(Also Part II, Sections 811(k), 1005, Regulations 105, Section 81.10.)

Reference(s): Code Sec. 2031 Reg § 20.2031-2

In valuing the stock of closely held corporations, or the stock of corporations where market quotations are not available, all other available financial data, as well as all relevant factors affecting the fair market value must be considered for estate tax and gift tax purposes. No general formula may be given that is applicable to the many different valuation situations arising in the valuation of such stock. However, the general approach, methods and factors which must be considered in valuing such securities are outlined.

Revenue Ruling 54-77, C.B. 1954-1, 187, superseded.

Sec. 1. Purpose.

The purpose of this Revenue Ruling is to outline and review in general the approach, methods and factors to be considered in valuing shares of the capital stock of closely held corporations for estate tax and gift tax purposes. The methods discussed herein will apply likewise to the valuation of corporate stocks on which market quotations are either unavailable or are of such scarcity that they do not reflect the fair market value.

Sec. 2. Background and Definitions.

.01 All valuations must be made in accordance with the applicable provisions of the Internal Revenue Code of 1954 and the Federal Estate Tax and Gift Tax Regulations. Sections 2031(a), 2032 and 2512(a) of the 1954 Code (sections 811 and 1005 of the 1939 Code) require that the property to be included in the gross estate, or made the subject of a gift, shall be taxed on the basis of the value of the property at the time of death of the decedent, the alternate date if so elected, or the date of gift.

.02 Section 20.2031-1(b) of the Estate Tax Regulations (section 81.10 of the Estate Tax Regulations 105) and section 25.2512-1 of the Gift Tax Regulations (section 86.19 of Gift Tax Regulations 108) define fair market value, in effect, as the price at which the property would change hands between a willing buyer and a willing seller when the former is not under any compulsion to buy and the latter is not under any compulsion to sell, both parties having reasonable knowledge of relevant facts. Court decisions frequently state in addition that the hypothetical buyer and seller are assumed to be able, as well as willing, to trade and to be well informed about the property and concerning the market for such property.

.03 Closely held corporations are those corporations the shares of which are owned by a relatively limited number of stockholders. Often the entire stock issue is held by one family. The result of this situation is that little, if any, trading in the shares takes place. There is, therefore, no established market for the stock and such sales as occur at irregular intervals seldom reflect all of the elements of a representative transaction as defined by the term "fair market value."

Sec. 3. Approach to Valuation.

.01 A determination of fair market value, being a question of fact, will depend upon the circumstances in each case. No formula can be devised that will be generally applicable to the multitude of different valuation issues arising in estate and gift tax cases. Often, an appraiser will find wide differences of opinion as to the fair market value of a particular stock. In resolving such differences, he should maintain a reasonable attitude in recognition of the fact that valuation is not an exact science. A sound valuation will be based upon all the relevant facts, but the elements of common sense, informed judgment and reasonableness must enter into the process of weighing those facts and determining their aggregate significance.

.02 The fair market value of specific shares of stock will vary as general economic conditions change from "normal" to "boom" or "depression," that is, according to the degree of optimism or pessimism with which the investing public regards the future at the required date of appraisal. Uncertainty as to the stability or continuity of the future income from a property decreases its value by increasing the risk of loss of earnings and value in the future. The value of shares of stock of a company with very uncertain future prospects is highly speculative. The appraiser must exercise his judgment as to the degree of risk attaching to the business of the corporation which issued the stock, but that judgment must be related to all of the other factors affecting value.

.03 Valuation of securities is, in essence, a prophesy as to the future and must be based on facts available at the required date of appraisal. As a generalization, the prices of stocks which are traded in volume in a free and active market by informed persons best reflect the consensus of the investing public as to what the future holds for the corporations and industries represented. When a stock is closely held, is traded infrequently, or is traded in an erratic market, some other measure of value must be used. In many instances, the next best measure may be found in the prices at which the stocks of companies engaged in the same or a similar line of business are selling in a free and open market.

Sec. 4. Factors to Consider.

.01 It is advisable to emphasize that in the valuation of the stock of closely held corporations or the stock of corporations where market quotations are either lacking or too scarce to be recognized, all available financial data, as well as all relevant factors affecting the fair market value, should be considered. The following factors, although not all-inclusive are fundamental and require careful analysis in each case:

(a) The nature of the business and the history of the enterprise from its inception.

(b) The economic outlook in general and the condition and outlook of the specific industry in particular.

(c) The book value of the stock and the financial condition of the business.

(d) The earning capacity of the company.

(e) The dividend-paying capacity.

(f) Whether or not the enterprise has goodwill or other intangible value.

(g) Sales of the stock and the size of the block of stock to be valued.

(h) The market price of stocks of corporations engaged in the same or a similar line of business having their stocks actively traded in a free and open market, either on an exchange or over-the-counter.

.02 The following is a brief discussion of each of the foregoing factors:

(a) The history of a corporate enterprise will show its past stability or instability, its growth or lack of growth, the diversity or lack of diversity of its operations, and other facts needed to form an opinion of the degree of risk involved in the business. For an enterprise which changed its form of organization but carried on the same or closely similar operations of its predecessor, the history of the former enterprise should be considered. The detail to be considered should increase with approach to the required date of appraisal, since recent events are of greatest help in predicting the future; but a study of gross and net income, and of dividends covering a long prior period, is highly desirable. The history to be studied should include, but need not be limited to, the nature of the business, its products or services, its operating and investment assets, capital structure, plant facilities, sales records and management, all of which should be considered as of the date of the appraisal, with due regard for recent significant changes. Events of the past that are unlikely to recur in the future should be discounted, since value has a close relation to future expectancy.

(b) A sound appraisal of a closely held stock must consider current and prospective economic conditions as of the date of appraisal, both in the national economy and in the industry or industries with which the corporation is allied. It is important to know that the company is more or less successful than its competitors in the same industry, or that it is maintaining a stable position with respect to competitors. Equal or even greater significance may attach to the ability of the industry with which the company is allied to compete with other industries. Prospective competition which has not been a factor in prior years should be given careful attention. For example, high profits due to the novelty of its product and the lack of competition often lead to increasing competition. The public's appraisal of the future prospects of competitive industries or of competitors within an industry may be indicated by price trends in the markets for commodities and for securities. The loss of the manager of a so-called "one-man" business may have a depressing effect upon the value of the stock of such business, particularly if there is a lack of trained personnel capable of succeeding to the management of the enterprise. In valuing the stock of this type of business, therefore, the effect of the loss of the manager on the future expectancy of the business, and the absence of management-succession potentialities are pertinent factors to be taken into consideration. On the other hand, there may be factors which offset, in whole or in part, the loss of the manager's services. For instance, the nature of the business and of its assets may be such that they will not be impaired by the loss of the manager. Furthermore, the loss may be adequately covered by life insurance, or competent management might be employed on the basis of the consideration paid for the former manager's services. These, or other offsetting factors, if found to exist, should be carefully weighed against the loss of the manager's services in valuing the stock of the enterprise.

(c) Balance sheets should be obtained, preferably in the form of comparative annual statements for two or more years immediately preceding the date of appraisal, together with a balance sheet at the end of the month preceding that date, if corporate accounting will permit. Any balance sheet descriptions that are not self-explanatory, and balance sheet items comprehending diverse assets or liabilities, should be clarified in essential detail by supporting supplemental schedules. These statements usually will disclose to the appraiser (1) liquid position (ratio of current assets to current liabilities); (2) gross and net book value of principal classes of fixed assets; (3) working capital; (4) long-term indebtedness; (5) capital structure; and (6) net worth. Consideration also should be given to any assets not essential to the operation of the business, such as investments in securities, real estate, etc. In general, such nonoperating assets will command a lower rate of return than do the operating assets, although in exceptional cases the reverse may be true. In computing the book value per share of stock, assets of the investment type should be revalued on the basis of their market price and the book value adjusted accordingly. Comparison of the company's balance sheets over several years may reveal, among other facts, such developments as the acquisition of additional production facilities or subsidiary companies, improvement in financial position, and details as to recapitalizations and other changes in the capital structure of the corporation. If the corporation has more than one class of stock outstanding, the charter or certificate of incorporation should be examined to ascertain the explicit rights and privileges of the various stock issues including: (1) voting powers, (2) preference as to dividends, and (3) preference as to assets in the event of liquidation.

(d) Detailed profit-and-loss statements should be obtained and considered for a representative period immediately prior to the required date of appraisal, preferably five or more years. Such statements should show (1) gross income by principal items; (2) principal deductions from gross income including major prior items of operating expenses, interest and other expense on each item of long-term debt, depreciation and depletion if such deductions are made, officers' salaries, in total if they appear to be reasonable or in detail if they seem to be excessive, contributions (whether or not deductible for tax purposes) that the nature of its business and its community position require the corporation to make, and taxes by principal items, including income and excess profits taxes; (3) net income available for dividends; (4) rates and amounts of dividends paid on each class of stock; (5) remaining amount carried to surplus; and (6) adjustments to, and reconciliation with, surplus as stated on the balance sheet. With profit and loss statements of this character available, the appraiser should be able to separate recurrent from nonrecurrent items of income and expense, to distinguish between operating income and investment income, and to ascertain whether or not any line of business in which the company is engaged is operated consistently at a loss and might be abandoned with benefit to the company. The percentage of earnings retained for business expansion should be noted when dividend-paying capacity is considered. Potential future income is a major factor in many valuations of closely held stocks, and all information concerning past income which will be helpful in predicting the future should be secured. Prior earnings records usually are the most reliable guide as to the future expectancy, but resort to arbitrary five- or ten-year averages without regard to current trends or future prospects will not produce a realistic valuation. If, for instance, a record of progressively increasing or decreasing net income is found, then greater weight may be accorded the most recent years' profits in estimating earning power. It will be helpful, in judging risk and the extent to which a business is a marginal operator, to consider deductions from income and net income in terms of percentage of sales. Major categories of cost and expense to be so analyzed include the consumption of raw materials and supplies in the case of manufacturers, processors and fabricators; the cost of purchased merchandise in the case of merchants; utility services; insurance; taxes; depletion or depreciation; and interest.

(e) Primary consideration should be given to the dividend-paying capacity of the company rather than to dividends actually paid in the past. Recognition must be given to the necessity of retaining a reasonable portion of profits in a company to meet competition. Dividend-paying capacity is a factor that must be considered in an appraisal, but dividends actually paid in the past may not have any relation to dividend-paying capacity. Specifically, the dividends paid by a closely held family company may be measured by the income needs of the stockholders or by their desire to avoid taxes on dividend receipts, instead of by the ability of the company to pay dividends. Where an actual or effective controlling interest in a corporation is to be valued, the dividend factor is not a material element, since the payment of such dividends is discretionary with the controlling stockholders. The individual or group in control can substitute salaries and bonuses for dividends, thus reducing net income and understating the dividend-paying capacity of the company. It follows, therefore, that dividends are less reliable criteria of fair market value than other applicable factors.

(f) In the final analysis, goodwill is based upon earning capacity. The presence of goodwill and its value, therefore, rests upon the excess of net earnings over and above a fair return on the net tangible assets. While the element of goodwill may be based primarily on earnings, such factors as the prestige and renown of the business, the ownership of a trade or brand name, and a record of successful operation over a prolonged period in a particular locality, also may furnish support for the inclusion of intangible value. In some instances it may not be possible to make a separate appraisal of the tangible and intangible assets of the business. The enterprise has a value as an entity. Whatever intangible value there is, which is supportable by the facts, may be measured by the amount by which the appraised value of the tangible assets exceeds the net book value of such assets.

(g) Sales of stock of a closely held corporation should be carefully investigated to determine whether they represent transactions at arm's length. Forced or distress sales do not ordinarily reflect fair market value nor do isolated sales in small amounts necessarily control as the measure of value. This is especially true in the valuation of a controlling interest in a corporation. Since, in the case of closely held stocks, no prevailing market prices are available, there is no basis for making an adjustment for blockage. It follows, therefore, that such stocks should be valued upon a consideration of all the evidence affecting the fair market value. The size of the block of stock itself is a relevant factor to be considered. Although it is true that a minority interest in an unlisted corporation's stock is more difficult to sell than a similar block of listed stock, it is equally true that control of a corporation, either actual or in effect, representing as it does an added element of value, may justify a higher value for a specific block of stock.

(h) Section 2031(b) of the Code states, in effect, that in valuing unlisted securities the value of stock or securities of corporations engaged in the same or a similar line of business which are listed on an exchange should be taken into consideration along with all other factors. An important consideration is that the corporations to be used for comparisons have capital stocks which are actively traded by the public. In accordance with section 2031(b) of the Code, stocks listed on an exchange are to be considered first. However, if sufficient comparable companies whose stocks are listed on an exchange cannot be found, other comparable companies which have stocks actively traded in on the over-the-counter market also may be used. The essential factor is that whether the stocks are sold on an exchange or over-the-counter there is evidence of an active, free public market for the stock as of the valuation date. In selecting corporations for comparative purposes, care should be taken to use only comparable companies. Although the only restrictive requirement as to comparable corporations specified in the statute is that their lines of business be the same or similar, yet it is obvious that consideration must be given to other relevant factors in order that the most valid comparison possible will be obtained. For illustration, a corporation having one or more issues of preferred stock, bonds or debentures in addition to its common stock should not be considered to be directly comparable to one having only common stock outstanding. In like manner, a company with a declining business and decreasing markets is not comparable to one with a record of current progress and market expansion.

Sec. 5. Weight to Be Accorded Various Factors.

The valuation of closely held corporate stock entails the consideration of all relevant factors as stated in section 4. Depending upon the circumstances in each case, certain factors may carry more weight than others because of the nature of the company's business. To illustrate:

(a) Earnings may be the most important criterion of value in some cases whereas asset value will receive primary consideration in others. In general, the appraiser will accord primary consideration to earnings when valuing stocks of companies which sell products or services to the public; conversely, in the investment or holding type of company, the appraiser may accord the greatest weight to the assets underlying the security to be valued.

(b) The value of the stock of a closely held investment or real estate holding company, whether or not family owned, is closely related to the value of the assets underlying the stock. For companies of this type the appraiser should determine the fair market values of the assets of the company. Operating expenses of such a company and the cost of liquidating it, if any, merit consideration when appraising the relative values of the stock and the underlying assets. The market values of the underlying assets give due weight to potential earnings and dividends of the particular items of property underlying the stock, capitalized at rates deemed proper by the investing public at the date of appraisal. A current appraisal by the investing public should be superior to the retrospective opinion of an individual. For these reasons, adjusted net worth should be accorded greater weight in valuing the stock of a closely held investment or real estate holding company, whether or not family owned, than any of the other customary yardsticks of appraisal, such as earnings and dividend paying capacity.

Sec. 6. Capitalization Rates.

In the application of certain fundamental valuation factors, such as earnings and dividends, it is necessary to capitalize the average or current results at some appropriate rate. A determination of the proper capitalization rate presents one of the most difficult problems in valuation. That there is no ready or simple solution will become apparent by a cursory check of the rates of return and dividend yields in terms of the selling prices of corporate shares listed on the major exchanges of the country. Wide variations will be found even for companies in the same industry. Moreover, the ratio will fluctuate from year to year depending upon economic conditions. Thus, no standard tables of capitalization rates applicable to closely held corporations can be formulated. Among the more important factors to be taken into consideration in deciding upon a capitalization rate in a particular case are: (1) the nature of the business; (2) the risk involved; and (3) the stability or irregularity of earnings.

Sec. 7. Average of Factors.

Because valuations cannot be made on the basis of a prescribed formula, there is no means whereby the various applicable factors in a particular case can be assigned mathematical weights in deriving the fair market value. For this reason, no useful purpose is served by taking an average of several factors (for example, book value, capitalized earnings and capitalized dividends) and basing the valuation on the result. Such a process excludes active consideration of other pertinent factors, and the end result cannot be supported by a realistic application of the significant facts in the case except by mere chance.

Sec. 8. Restrictive Agreements.

Frequently, in the valuation of closely held stock for estate and gift tax purposes, it will be found that the stock is subject to an agreement restricting its sale or transfer. Where shares of stock were acquired by a decedent subject to an option reserved by the issuing corporation to repurchase at a certain price, the option price is usually accepted as the fair market value for estate tax purposes. See Rev. Rul. 54-76, C.B. 1954-1, 194. However, in such case the option price is not determinative of fair market value for gift tax purposes. Where the option, or buy and sell agreement, is the result of voluntary action by the stockholders and is binding during the life as well as at the death of the stockholders, such agreement may or may not, depending upon the circumstances of each case, fix the value for estate tax purposes. However, such agreement is a factor to be considered, with other relevant factors, in determining fair market value. Where the stockholder is free to dispose of his shares during life and the option is to become effective only upon his death, the fair market value is not limited to the option price. It is always necessary to consider the relationship of the parties, the relative number of shares held by the decedent, and other material facts, to determine whether the agreement represents a bona fide business arrangement or is a device to pass the decedent's shares to the natural objects of his bounty for less than an adequate and full consideration in money or money's worth. In this connection see Rev. Rul. 157 C.B. 1953-2, 255, and Rev. Rul. 189, C.B. 1953-2, 294.

Sec. 9. Effect on Other Documents.

Revenue Ruling 54-77, C.B. 1954-1, 187, is hereby superseded.

Appendix C
Revenue Ruling 68-609

Rev. Rul. 68-609 1968-2 C.B. 327

IRS Headnote

The "formula" approach may be used in determining the fair market value of intangible assets of a business only if there is no better basis available for making the determination; A.R.M. 34, A.R.M. 68, O.D. 937, and Revenue Ruling 65-192 superseded. Ruling is to update and restate, under the current statute and regulations, the currently outstanding portions of A.R.M. 34, C.B. 2, 31 (1920), A.R.M. 68, C.B. 3, 43 (1920), and O.D. 937, C.B. 4, 43 (1921).

Rev. Rul. 68-609[47]

The question presented is whether the "formula" approach, the capitalization of earnings in excess of a fair rate of return on net tangible assets, may be used to determine the fair market value of the intangible assets of a business.

The "formula" approach may be stated as follows:

A percentage return on the average annual value of the tangible assets used in a business is determined, using a period of years (preferably not less than five) immediately prior to the valuation date. The amount of the percentage return on tangible assets, thus determined, is deducted from the average earnings of the business for such period and the remainder, if any, is considered to be the amount of the average annual earnings from the intangible assets of the business for the period. This amount (considered as the average annual earnings from intangibles), capitalized at a percentage of, say, 15 to 20 percent, is the value of the intangible assets of the business determined under the "formula" approach.

The percentage of return on the average annual value of the tangible assets used should be the percentage prevailing in the industry involved at the date of valuation, or (when the industry percentage is not available) a percentage of 8 to 10 percent may be used.

---

47. Prepared pursuant to Rev. Proc. 67-6, C.B. 1967-1, 576.

The 8 percent rate of return and the 15 percent rate of capitalization are applied to tangibles and intangibles, respectively, of businesses with a small risk factor and stable and regular earnings; the 10 percent rate of return and 20 percent rate of capitalization are applied to businesses in which the hazards of business are relatively high.

The above rates are used as examples and are not appropriate in all cases. In applying the "formula" approach, the average earnings period and the capitalization rates are dependent upon the facts pertinent thereto in each case.

The past earnings to which the formula is applied should fairly reflect the probable future earnings. Ordinarily, the period should not be less than five years, and abnormal years, whether above or below the average, should be eliminated. If the business is a sole proprietorship or partnership, there should be deducted from the earnings of the business a reasonable amount for services performed by the owner or partners engaged in the business. See *Lloyd B. Sanderson Estate v. Commissioner*, 42 F.2d 160 (1930). Further, only the tangible assets entering into net worth, including accounts and bills receivable in excess of accounts and bills payable, are used for determining earnings on the tangible assets. Factors that influence the capitalization rate include (1) the nature of the business, (2) the risk involved, and (3) the stability or irregularity of earnings.

The "formula" approach should not be used if there is better evidence available from which the value of intangibles can be determined. If the assets of a going business are sold upon the basis of a rate of capitalization that can be substantiated as being realistic, though it is not within the range of figures indicated here as the ones ordinarily to be adopted, the same rate of capitalization should be used in determining the value of intangibles.

Accordingly, the "formula" approach may be used for determining the fair market value of intangible assets of a business only if there is no better basis therefor available.

See also Revenue Ruling 59-60, C.B. 1959-1, 237, as modified by Revenue Ruling 65-193, C.B. 1965-2, 370, which sets forth the proper approach to use in the valuation of closely held corporate stocks for estate and gift tax purposes. The general approach, methods and factors, outlined in Revenue Ruling 59-60, as modified, are equally applicable to valuations of corporate stocks for income and other tax purposes as well as for estate and gift tax purposes. They apply also to problems involving the determination of the fair market value of business interests of any type, including partnerships and proprietorships, and of intangible assets for all tax purposes.

A.R.M. 34, A.R.M. 68, and O.D. 937 are superseded, since the positions set forth therein are restated to the extent applicable under current law in this Revenue Ruling. Revenue Ruling 65-192, C.B. 1965-2, 259, which contained restatements of A.R.M. 34 and A.R.M. 68, is also superseded.

Index